God's Whisper in a Mother's CHAOS

BRINGING PEACE HOME

Keri Wyatt Kent

Foreword by Lynne Hybels

InterVarsity Press
Downers Grove, Illinois

InterVarsity Press
P.O. Box 1400, Downers Grove, IL 60515
World Wide Web: www.ivpress.com
E-mail: mail@ivpress.com

*InterVarsity Press® is the book-publishing division of InterVarsity Christian Fellowship/USA®, a student
movement active on campus at hundreds of universities, colleges and schools of nursing in the United States
of America, and a member movement of the International Fellowship of Evangelical Students. For
information about local and regional activities, write Public Relations Dept., InterVarsity Christian
Fellowship/USA, 6400 Schroeder Rd., P.O. Box 7895, Madison, WI 53707-7895.*

All Scripture quotations, unless otherwise indicated, are taken from the Holy Bible, New International
Version®. NIV®. *Copyright* ©*1973, 1978, 1984 by International Bible Society. Used by permission of
Zondervan Publishing House. All rights reserved.*

Cover photograph: Tetsuya Miura/Photonica
Chapter headings: Roberta Polfus

ISBN 0-8308-2270-4

Printed in the United States of America ∞

Library of Congress Cataloging-in-Publication Data

Kent, Keri Wyatt, 1963-
    God's whisper in a mother's chaos: bringing peace home/Keri Wyatt Kent.
      p. cm.
    Includes bibliographical references.
    ISBN 0-8308-2270-4 (paper: alk. paper)
      1. Mothers—Religious life. 2. Motherhood—Religious aspects—Christianity. I. Title.

  BV4529.18.K47 2000
  248.8'431—dc21
                                                       00-039578

| 20 | 19 | 18 | 17 | 16 | 15 | 14 | 13 | 12 | 11 | 10 | 9 | 8 | 7 | 6 | 5 |
| 16 | 15 | 14 | 13 | 12 | 11 | 10 | 09 | 08 | 07 | 06 | 05 | 04 | | | |

To Scot, Melanie and Aaron,
without whom my life
would have considerably less chaos . . .
and significantly less joy

CONTENTS

Foreword

I was delighted as I read *God's Whisper in a Mother's Chaos* to discover that many of the themes running through Keri's book are the very themes I am currently focusing on in my own life. As a middle-aged mother enjoying the relative freedom of the empty nest, my daily life looks very different from that of a young mother of preschoolers, yet in our spiritual lives Keri and I seem to be running on parallel tracks. Why? Because we hold in common the simple belief that nothing in life is more important than learning to listen to the whisper of God.

Do we need wisdom? Then listen to the whisper. Do we need to feel loved? Then listen to the whisper. Do we need rest and refreshment? Then listen to the whisper. Do we need to be challenged and changed? Then listen to the whisper.

It sounds simple enough, but the truth is that most of us are poor listeners. Listening requires an uncluttered mind, and most of us allow our minds to become as cluttered as our kitchen counters. And sadly if we have a moment or an hour to devote to uncluttering, we will probably attend to the kitchen counter rather than to our minds. It has taken me decades to realize the clutter that fills my mind is a far more serious problem than the clutter that fills my house.

What is it that clutters our minds and keeps us from hearing the whisper of God? For some of us it's a distorted view of God. For years such clutter filled my mind. I had grown up seeing God as a harsh taskmaster whose love I had to earn by working hard, by keeping busy, by striving, striving, striving. Could I sit quietly and just *be* in the presence of God, as Keri suggests in this book? Certainly not!

But the god in my mind was not the God of Scripture. The God Keri describes is the true God, the God who longs for us to slow down, be quiet and let him love us. This is the God who says to a young mother weary of the mundane, "When no one else sees what you do, I see, and I value it." This is the God who says to a young mother overwhelmed by her sinfulness, "Yes, today you failed to love as I would have you love. But I offer you forgiveness and a fresh start tomorrow. Rest tonight in my favor."

A distorted view of God is not all that clutters our minds. Keri writes about the clutter of guilt, about our unwillingness to trust, and about our failure to recognize God's voice as he speaks through the events and the people that fill our daily lives. In gentle tones she invites us to join her on a journey through the clutter so that we can find the freedom to "drink in God's love for us."

There are two things I particularly like about this book. One, it is written in the present tense. Most authors write of their early mothering years long after their kids have traded diapers for designer jeans and a bottle of milk for a Diet Coke. But Keri wrote this book with preschoolers playing—or sleeping or fighting or laughing or whining—in the background. The result is a realistic book. She knows what a young mom can manage and what she can't. So it's a short book, it gets right to the point, and it offers practical suggestions.

The other thing I like is that this book is balanced. Keri writes of both our need to embrace the chaos of our lives and of our need to withdraw from it at times. She writes of our need to accept both the comforts of grace and the challenges of growth. ("Are we," she asks, "becoming more like Jesus?") She writes both of making more space in our closets and making more space in our hearts for God. She writes of creating beauty in our homes through attitudes of peace and joy as well as through our attention to cleanliness and decor. She writes both of our need to be faithful to the high and demanding call of motherhood and of our need to develop and use the spiritual gifts God has placed within us. She challenges us both to service and solitude, and claims, again with a mother's realism, that we can be devoted to both.

The balance in Keri's book flows naturally from the balance in her life. Of course, she would not want me to claim for her the achievement of perfect balance; she would certainly not claim it for herself. And yet the respect she has earned in the marketplace, her devotion as a wife and mother, and her faithful service for many years at Willow Creek Community Church are all testimonies to the very real work of God in all dimensions of her life. It is that "very real work of God" that has given birth to this book.

Lynne Hybels

Acknowledgments

Lee Strobel: Thanks for cheering me on. Your mentoring and encouragement helped me start this book. Your courageous example of what it means to follow God's holy calling helped me to finish it.

Bob Gordon: Thank you for your insightful editing, encouragement and friendship, all of which bring out the best in my writing. This book would never have happened without your wise counsel and encouraging challenge.

Deb Beise: Thanks for your generous help and for your Christlike example of courage in the midst of chaos.

Mom and Dad: Your love and godly example provided a firm foundation of faith in my life. I love you!

Special thanks to Robin McLennan, Teresa Nortillo, Sue Cole, Gina Young and Lynn Siewert for encouraging me and believing in me when I was so uncertain about myself and about the future of this book. Each of you has blessed me with your friendship.

1
· · · · ·

Embracing
the Chaos

It is the longest hour of the day, before my little ones succumb to sleep. My husband is working late again, and I am going from room to room, soothing, singing, rocking, threatening—and I have only two children!

"Mommy, will you tell me a story? Not a reading story, a telling story that you make up?" pleads the three year old from her bed in a sweet voice with just the slightest edge of a whine.

"Mommy, sit in chair me!" demands the toddler, who a moment earlier was downstairs crying because I wouldn't pick up his blankie for him. "Cuddle, cuddle," he implores, patting the La-Z-Boy, clutching his blankie and looking up at

me with irresistible blue eyes. How could a child so exasper-
ating one moment be so endearing the next? Even so, in moments like this I fantasize about having a nanny or a clone or
a husband with a nine-to-five job. I can't afford the nanny,
the clone thing would just be too weird, and I'm not holding
my breath on my husband having his evenings free. His long
hours are typical, I suppose, of anyone working on straight
commission to support a family. It's part of the tradeoff for
the privilege I have of being home with my kids. But at times
like this I am tired and frustrated and feeling anything but
privileged.

An hour later the children are snoring cherubs, and my
toes are getting prunelike from a hot bubble bath. By the
time I emerge from the tub, my anger has cooled like the
bath water, leaving in its place a soap-scum ring of loneliness
and self-pity—and plenty of self-doubt.

I used to handle intense on-the-job pressure at a daily
newspaper and stay cool. I actually enjoyed the adrenaline
rush of dealing with demanding editors, tight deadlines, the
noise and chaos of the newsroom. I could interview powerful
politicians and pound out a breaking news story in a busy
newsroom. So why can't I handle bedtime with two people
less than three feet tall? What's happened to me?

I wish my husband were home. I wish my kids were angelic
more often, instead of only when they're sleeping or when
they think I'm not looking. I wish I had more of God's peace
and strength.

Where is God in the midst of the chaos that is my life, I
wonder? I wish I could feel his gentle presence when the

sudden storms that rage through each of my days hit me head-on. I wish he could be here to tuck in my three year old.

On better nights, when the kids are more cooperative and I'm calmer, he does seem to be here. I hear my daughter's sweet bedtime prayer: "Dear Jesus, could you please just sleep with me tonight? I'm a little scared," and know that she is already becoming aware of his presence.

My children often understand the truth about God better than I. "Jesus is right here with us," I tell my daughter. Because I am her mother, she accepts and believes this—after asking a few more questions, as always! But do I believe it? Do I allow myself to be aware of God's presence? He is always here but not always acknowledged. He is always at the door but not always invited in.

In the crowded house that is my life, crammed full of the needs, demands and even the joys of my work, my children, my husband, my friends, how do I make room for God? When I feel pulled in so many different directions, how can I get centered? How can I live in God's presence? How can I hear the whisper of his gentle voice above the chaos of my life?

"Life is difficult," writes Scott Peck in *The Road Less Traveled.* "Once we truly know that life is difficult—once we truly understand and accept it—then life is no longer difficult. Because once it is accepted, the fact that life is difficult no longer matters."

In fact, God uses the chaos to sanctify us, that is, to make us more like Jesus. I know, because I have often asked God questions like "Why is this parenting thing so hard? Why does normal daily life have to be such a struggle?" When I come to the end of my questions, if I strain the ears of my heart to listen, I sometimes hear him whisper, "So that Christ may be more fully formed in you."

Resisting the chaos in our lives hinders the work of God in our souls. When we embrace the chaos, admit that it is there and it is okay because God is there too, then the difficulties and unpredictable circumstances of our lives become a tool that God uses to strengthen our faith.

Looking for Peace

Is it possible to find the eye of the hurricane of your life? Plenty of self-help books or self-appointed spiritual gurus would say simply, "Look within yourself," and although that sounds good, it is not enough. Alone, looking within, all I see is more chaos, a confusing mixture of good intentions and selfish desires that don't ultimately bring me peace.

Jesus said, "My peace I give you. I do not give to you as the world gives" (Jn 14:27).

Jesus said, "Come to me . . . and I will give you rest" (Mt 11:28).

So how do we go to Jesus? How do we get the peace and rest that he promises? In the cacophony of voices that shout for our attention, how do we discern which is his?

Hearing God's voice requires a new way of listening, a new way of seeing. In my life that perspective was often provided by the chaos itself. When I am able to see difficulties and everyday struggles as God's way of honing my character, I am better able to appreciate the lessons that life's messy and chaotic moments have to offer.

But that is only half of the equation. If I intentionally with-draw from the chaos on a regular basis, I am a more patient mother, a more loving wife and a gentler person. By spending time alone with God, I allow him to care for my soul so that I can better care for those he has entrusted to me. If I go away for ten minutes, for two hours, for a day, I can better appreciate the lessons of the chaotic times. I can also learn more about being content in spite of my circumstances.

I do not always hear God's whisper. Usually I am at one of two extremes: overwhelmed by the chaos of being home with two small children, or complaining about the boredom of being home with two small children. It's an isolating paradox.

Sometimes, when the pendulum swings toward boredom, I unwittingly overcommit myself: scheduling play dates and volunteer activities with reckless abandon, taking on extra work projects. As a result, my life's pace becomes more frantic. That way, I can avoid the sometimes-frightening silence where I must dwell before I can hear God's whisper.

But then the pendulum swings back, and I find myself bogged down in the daily-ness of life. I get mired in routine, and I forget to live intentionally. I putter about, reacting to whatever seems urgent or just in my path, never finding, or making, time for the things that really matter.

This book details what I am learning about living in God's presence, about hearing his whisper in the midst of my chaos, and the questions I am bumping up against in the process. I am writing not as an expert but as a journalist, a student of life. As such, this is an investigative report, a research paper by a fellow traveler. It's a journey that I am taking even as I write it. If you are straining to hear that still, small voice, I invite you to come along on the journey and see where God takes us.

Making the "Practice" More Practical

A few years ago I was leading a small group in which we studied the Bible and Christian literature and tried to apply what we learned to our lives. One of the more interesting books we looked at is *The Practice of the Presence of God* by Brother Lawrence. This collection of letters from a quiet monk about how to live in God's presence moment by moment has changed the lives of many Christians, including mine. But with all due respect to Brother Lawrence, his life in a seventeenth-century monastery was vastly different than mine in twenty-first-century suburbia.

"He was a monk," objected one woman in our group. "How hard is it to think about God all the time if you're a monk?"

Indeed. But never having been one, I can't answer that, except to say that it was probably harder than we think, otherwise Brother Lawrence's book would not have endured as it has. But comparisons of who is busier, who has more entries in their daily planner, who works more hours, who has more children or has the more difficult children are simply ways of avoiding the real issue. How can I live in the presence of God in the midst of my hectic, busy life? How can I listen for the whisper of God's still, small voice in the chaos?

To answer that, I need to think about God himself. What

does his voice sound like? What is my perception of him? Who is he, and who am I, and why do I even want to hear his voice? With that question, our journey begins.

Getting the Most out of This Book

While writing this book I kept running into people whose lives were truly chaotic, much more than mine. They were facing huge, difficult trials that I have not experienced: infertility, cancer, the death of a child . . . the list goes on and on. I often asked myself, "What do I know about chaos? My life is peaceful compared to the lives of these people!"

Perhaps you feel the same way. But whether your life is just occasionally overwhelming or truly painful, you will always be able to find someone who is worse off—or better off—than you. Comparisons are not helpful. God doesn't use them.

No matter where you are and what you are experiencing, God wants to whisper to you: "I love you, my beloved child. I will never leave you. When you walk through the waters, you will not be drowned. When you walk through the flames, you will not be burned. For I am with you" (see Isaiah 43).

It is my prayer that you will be encouraged by this book to live in God's presence moment by moment, no matter what the chaos of your life looks like.

As you go through this book, the questions at the end of each chapter will help you process these big questions. They are for personal reflection or group discussion.

For Reflection

1. What three things add to the chaos of your life? Do these dis-

tract you from your relationship with God or draw you toward him?

2. "Life is difficult," writes Scott Peck in *The Road Less Traveled.*
"Once we truly know that life is difficult—once we truly understand
and accept it—then life is no longer difficult. Because once it is accepted, the fact that life is difficult no longer matters." Do you
agree? Why or why not?

3. When has God used everyday chaos or a difficult situation to
sanctify you? What did you learn?

2

. . . . .

Knowing the One
Who Whispers

*I*f *God spoke, what do you think he would sound like? The* deep, booming voice that pronounces the "thou shalt nots" to Moses in the movie *The Ten Commandments?* A wilting, vague, grandfatherly voice that offers flowery platitudes that sound spiritual but lack substance? Or maybe like a dissatisfied client calling your office with a list of complaints about your job performance?

God's voice has sounded different to me in different stages of my life. How I perceive him has to do more with me than with God. When I rebelled against him, his voice seemed ominous. When I drew close to God, it seemed gentle.

The Bible describes God's voice as powerful. And gentle.

And authoritative. And all of these things together.

Psalm 29:3-4, for example, talks about the voice of the Lord.

> The God of Glory thunders,
>   the LORD thunders over the mighty waters.
> The voice of the LORD is powerful:
>   the voice of the LORD is majestic.

David's psalm continues to elaborate on God's strong and powerful voice for several verses. But the concluding verse (v. 11) caught me off guard:

> The LORD gives strength to his people;
>   the LORD blesses his people with peace.

All that power, and yet the strength is not used against his people but given to them. He gives them strength and peace. God's power is a power of protection, a power that pours out peace, like a thunderstorm on parched, dry land.

In the Gospels, Jesus describes himself as a gentle and good shepherd. "His sheep follow him because they know his voice," Jesus says in John 10:1-17. "I am the good shepherd. I know my sheep and my sheep know me."

When I balance the two perspectives of these passages, what I hear is a voice of quiet authority, gentle leadership and unlimited yet self-restrained power.

I remember seeing a graphic illustration of this type of power while flipping through a magazine one day. A stark black-and-white photo caught my eye. You've probably seen this photo or one like it: an exquisitely muscled young man, bare to the waist, his chiseled biceps and pecs bulging, abs rippled. But he's not flexing in a typical bodybuilder's pose.

His head is bowed, so you can't see his face. He's holding a tiny, naked baby gently in his muscular arms. It's a perfect picture of power and strength restrained by love. The picture makes me think of God.

I can't hear God's voice above the din in my life if I don't know what to listen for. His voice, as the psalm tells me, is majestic and powerful. But it is not a power that intimidates or dominates. It is a power tempered by gentleness.

There's a wonderful passage in 1 Kings 19 that describes God's gentle side. The story is of the prophet Elijah who retreats to a mountain cave after a particularly trying series of events in his ministry.

God tells Elijah to stand on the mountain because the presence of the Lord is about to pass by (v. 11). The text then describes wind, earthquake and fire, but after each of these, it says, "the LORD was not in the wind," and "the LORD was not in the earthquake," and "the LORD was not in the fire" (v. 12).

So where was the Lord?

"And after the fire came a gentle whisper" (v. 12). And that's how God spoke to Elijah. God showed Elijah his power, but he spoke in a whisper.

Sometimes we expect an earthquake, and we miss his whisper. We expect a divine smack in the head, so we're oblivious to the divinity in the touch of our child's hand in ours as we cross the street.

Our perception, or misperception, of God can distort his voice. If you want to hear God's whisper, begin by paying attention to who he really is and who you see yourself to be in relationship to him.

Unpacking Our Baggage

Part of my skewed perception of God is a result of the baggage I carry with me from the past.

Some of us grew up with a view of God as a somber, finger-pointing judge. We see ourselves as condemned criminals or, at least, violators of divine will. And indeed, on one hand we are. But we see only the just side of God and are so afraid or intimidated that we are blind to his other side, the side that pours grace and mercy all over us. We don't realize how distorted our one-dimensional view of him is.

Or we hear that Jesus suffered and died for us, so we figure he's expecting payback for the rest of our lives.

Maybe for you he's like a demanding boss: ready to give you a bad review if you don't work hard enough or jump through the right hoops or meet your quota.

But the Bible describes God not as a boss but as a gentle shepherd. Sometimes that is hard for me to imagine. I mean, I can sing a song about the Good Shepherd in church or read verses in the Bible about him. But do I really see God as gentle and caring, who watches out for my best interest and will nurture and protect me? In a world where everyone is asking, "What have you done for me lately?" I sometimes imagine God asks me the same thing.

Many of us grew up trying to please God by avoiding certain sins, going to church, serving in charities or church groups, reading the Bible, having a formulaic "quiet time" on a regular basis and feeling guilty when we didn't. We think the only way to be "close to God" is to sit down for two hours early in the morning and pore over Scripture and pray as formally as we possibly can. You know, "Oh, Lord, Thou art *blah, blah, blah* . . . I thank Thee, Oh Lord, *blah, blah, blah* . . ."

It's true, prayer and church and Scripture memory are absolutely essential. But I confess, I have often undertaken such disciplines with impure motives. I am often more focused on doing my duty, or making some kind of impression on God, than on actually building a relationship with him.

Others of us feel we were such terrible sinners before we knew God that, although we are pretty sure he's forgiven us, we're relatively certain he doesn't really want to talk to us today. We feel like we got admission to heaven on a technicality; meanwhile we live in a self-made purgatory.

Sometimes, as a result of these distortions, I decide I need to earn a few divine merit badges. That's when I end up saying yes to too many things: writing just one more article, volunteering just once a month in the children's church, leading just one more group . . . I secretly hope that God and other people will be impressed. But I'm learning that he's not. Certainly he's glad that I'm giving and being diligent. But when my diligence becomes a way to avoid intimate connection with God, my life becomes more chaotic.

God, I have been surprised to learn lately, desires intimacy in the midst of chaos. And really, I want that too. As much as he wants me to find the time to come away to pray for more than a few moments, he knows that may not happen every day, at least while my children are still preschoolers. So in the meantime, I think, he'd like to do life with me, to be next to me as I drive the carpool, meet with a client or wash the dishes.

Another surprise: God cares more about who I am than what I do. And in his view, this is who I am: his beloved child, through no merit of my own, but because of his grace. Freed by glimpses into this truth, I am learning to tear down the walls I've carefully constructed around my definition of "time with God."

It seems that true connection requires me to embrace this truth: it is Christ's work on my behalf, not my own efforts, that bring me into his presence. Connection with God is about focusing on God and what I can give to him, not what I can get from him. Paradoxically, this kind of unselfishness brings me joy.

At our church the first half of the midweek service typically consists of worship and prayerful reflection. When I am in the right frame of mind, I focus on God. I give him my worship, like a present, like a command performance. I think about singing and praying just to him, the King of the universe. When I do this, I experience joy. Freedom.

But if I come to worship entangled in my own little problems, or thinking about what I can get out of worship, or thinking about how my voice sounds to the people around me, I miss out on joy. Bondage.

When I pray, it's the same. When I focus on God and not my own little laundry list of requests and complaints, I feel closer to him. I come into his presence. Freedom.

Self-Aware or Selfish?

The more I understand who God is, the more I desire to be with him. That this opportunity is available is amazing. Yet I take it for granted.

My ability to hear God's voice is hindered when my self-awareness teeters toward self-obsession.

Self-awareness is touted as a strength in our culture, but when I am too highly aware of myself, I impede my own prayers. Prayer that transforms, that brings me into God's presence, is focused on God. When I become too self-aware or self-conscious, prayer becomes empty ritual and ceases to be conversation.

My husband and I, like most couples, have disagreements. He tends to worry (he sees it as just being realistic), I tend to be an "it-will-all-work-out" type (I see it as having the gift of faith). I am very aware of this character trait, and frankly, I see it as a strength. But when my self-awareness becomes selfishness, I accuse him of being short of faith. From there I have only a short slide down the slippery slope to self-righteous pride. My self-awareness trips me up. It doesn't bring me closer to God or, for that matter, to the person I love most on this earth.

Like most busy moms, I often talk to myself. I don't know why. Maybe it's an indication of how desperate I can get for adult conversation. I'll actually be carrying on a conversation with myself, and suddenly I'll become self-aware, and then, quite quickly, self-conscious, especially if other people are around. Was I musing aloud?

Likewise, sometimes when I pray, I think too much about the prayer, wondering if God is listening and feeling rather self-conscious. At that point, it's not a conversation.

Instead, I'll start thinking in circles: *How good that I am praying. I so rarely get a minute to myself; it's so great to be able to pray. Isn't it good that here I am, praying. "Dear God, thanks that I can pray." Now let's see, what shall I pray about . . .*

I think more honest conversations come when both my kids are crying and I'm at the end of my rope and I say, "Lord, help me not to say or do something I'll regret, because these kids are driving me crazy!" It's not structured or neat, and it doesn't follow some cute little pattern for remembering how to pray. It's a "help!" prayer, and it gets heard. Not that I want all of my connections with God to have this tone. But it's freeing to know that no matter what I say to God, he hears me. I don't need formality or perfection or even a good attitude to touch the heart of God. It's also quite comforting to know, as Brennan Manning says, "When we try to pray and cannot, or when we fail in a sincere attempt to be compassionate, God touches us tenderly in return" (*The Ragamuffin Gospel*).

An Invitation You Wouldn't Refuse

Amazingly, God desires intimacy with you and with me. He wants to touch us tenderly, to whisper to us in the midst of our chaos. But it is hard to imagine that sometimes. He does not seem available to us.

Why? The answer, I think, is that God is not physically visible to us. But he can be quite real to us if we change the way we think about him.

If Billy Graham wrote and asked if he and Ruth could have dinner at my house the next time they come through Chicago, I would cancel almost anything to be able to welcome them to my home. Why? Because I feel that these people, as spiritual leaders, would help me to grow and learn. From them I would hope to gain insight and wisdom, strength and encouragement.

If the Creator of the entire universe said, "Can I have breakfast with you every day? Can we walk together as you go through your daily routines? Can I encourage and guide you?" What would I say? I'd want to say yes. And that is what he's asking, but so often I say, "Sounds good. I'll call you sometime." I put him off. Because I don't realize what a privilege it is to be able to just talk to God, I take it for granted.

Seeing Ourselves as God Does

I think the reason I do take him for granted and say I don't have time for spiritual pursuits is because I do not see myself as God sees me: deeply loved. I do not even hear his invitation, or I assume it is for other people.

Henri J. M. Nouwen wrote his book *Life of the Beloved* for a friend who was curious about spiritual matters. Nouwen tells him that God sees him, as he does all people, as "the Beloved." How hard it is, even though I profess faith in God, to know and believe this. But if I want to hear God's whisper, I need to have this truth permeate my self-perception, to completely soak through the fabric of my being.

When I read Nouwen's words, I began to see God in a new way:

> Yes, there is that voice, the voice that speaks from above and from within and that whispers softly or declares loudly: "You are my Beloved, on you my favor rests." It certainly is not easy to hear that voice in a world filled with voices that shout: "You

are no good, you are ugly; you are worthless; you are despicable, you are nobody—unless you can demonstrate the opposite." These negative voices are so loud and so persistent that it is easy to believe them. That's the great trap. It is the trap of self-rejection.

We so often fool ourselves into believing that the self-rejection Nouwen refers to is actually, at least in our case, merely humility. But if I reject my identity—precious child of God because of Christ—I am not humble but deceived. My spiritual growth is hindered, because I am not partaking of the greatest spiritual food in the world: God's abundant love.

You are the beloved. You may feel humbled by this; I know I do. "Why me?" you and I may ask. You can rest assured that it is by no merit of yours. God created you and has loved you since the beginning of time, and nothing you do can change that.

God does not judge you based on what you have or have not done. He looks at you through Jesus. What does that mean? If you have put your trust in Christ to forgive and lead you, God does not see your sin. He sees your new, forgiven self. And no matter where you are on your spiritual journey, he is completely in love with you.

In one of Jesus' best-known parables, the story of the prodigal son, Jesus attempts to paint a picture of what God is like. Despite the heartbreaking rebellion of his son, the father in the story hopes that his son will return. Eventually the sinful son comes crawling back. Most of us would expect the father to make him pay back the money he had squandered, or at least give his son a long lecture. But that is not what happens. The father throws a party and rejoices that the son he thought was lost forever is now alive and with him. Although I've known the story since childhood, it never ceases to amaze me.

It's difficult to imagine God as a father who runs to hug us when we screw up. But if we don't see God as he truly is, our communication with him is hindered. We don't hear his voice—not because he is not speaking—but because we don't expect it to be so gentle, so full of grace and forgiveness.

> What blocks forgiveness is not God's reticence . . . but ours. God's arms are always extended; we are the ones who turn away. . . . I have meditated enough on Jesus' stories of grace to let their meaning filter through. Still, each time I confront their astonishing message I realize how thickly the veil of ungrace obscures my view of God. (Philip Yancey, *What's So Amazing About Grace?*)

God loves me. He loves you. Not just in an obligatory way, because he's supposed to. He is crazy about you. Even if you want nothing to do with him, he longs for you. He wants to be with you, not just to hear you praise him or thank him, but to comfort and nurture you, like a parent. A perfect parent.

"On our own, would any of us come up with the notion of a God who loves and yearns to be loved?" Yancey writes in *The Jesus I Never Knew.* "Those raised in a Christian tradition may miss the shock of Jesus' message, but in truth love has never been a normal way of describing what happens between human beings and their God. Not once does the Qur'an apply the word love to God."

He is a God who yearns to be loved. And I am his precious child, whom he adores. When I catch sight of these two simple yet profound truths, I begin to shift the paradigm. From the starting point of who he truly is, I can begin to see that he can be trusted.

God really does have my best interests at heart. His power protects me and will not hurt me. But the next step of my journey would test my ability to trust him and bring me through a type of chaos unlike any I'd experienced before.

For Reflection

1. "O Jerusalem, Jerusalem, you who kill the prophets and stone those sent to you, how often I have longed to gather your children together, as a hen gathers her chicks under her wings, but you were not willing!" (Lk 13:34). Jesus is talking about his people. What does it mean to be "gathered under Jesus' wings"? What gets in the way of your willingness to let Jesus do just that?

2. Write down "When God thinks about me, he thinks . . ." Then write down what comes to mind. If your list is mostly past sins and shortcomings, read the story of the prodigal son in Luke 15.

Notice how the father focuses not on past sins but on reconciliation. Add words like *special* and *a treasure* to your list. If you find it hard to believe that God sees you in this way, what are some steps that you could take to grow in this area?

3. "How thickly the veil of ungrace obscures my view of God," writes Philip Yancey. What ungrace in your life obscures your view of God?

4. Think about the prodigal seasons in your life. What temptations pulled you away from God? What brought you back? Did you experience forgiveness like the prodigal son did, or did your guilt and shame cause you to miss grace?

3

· · · · ·

Learning
to Trust

I t was a quiet February afternoon. I was in the kitchen with my
daughter, who was twenty-two months old at the time. I
was awkwardly attempting to empty the dishwasher
while she was trying to "help" me. I was more than eight
months pregnant and growing increasingly frustrated over
the challenge of what should have been a simple task. Finally
I sat Melanie down at the table with a coloring book and
crayons and was just turning back to the dishwasher when I
heard the downstairs door open and shut.

"Scot?" I called. There was no answer. I glanced at the
clock: not yet three o'clock. I walked downstairs. "What are
you doing home?"

He dropped a cardboard box full of files, framed photos and a coffee mug on the floor, looked down at them, then looked up at me, his eyes desperate, defeated. "Sears had a layoff today. I lost my job." His words hung in the air for a moment as I stared at him in disbelief.

"Oh, honey . . ." I put my arms around him. But as I reflexively reached to comfort him, my head spun with panicked questions. *Why is this happening? I'm having a baby in a few weeks! God, where are you?*

Two weeks later our son was born. Scot was home sending out résumés for the first month or two after Aaron arrived. Overwhelmed by the stress of our circumstances and trying to care for two children in diapers, I leaned heavily on him. Concerned about the future of our family and our financial situation, he leaned right back. But Scot was at home, and that was just one of the blessings hidden in this trial.

A job Scot had hoped for didn't turn out. He decided to change careers and sell real estate full-time, an interest he had dabbled in for a few years.

So here we were, with a severance package that was running out, my husband in a straight commission job in a new field and me at home with two babies. It was more than I felt capable of handling. I tried to keep up a strong outward appearance, but I was drowning inside. I felt depressed, sad and lonely. And I felt like a wimp because of how I felt. I had always been strong, and now I just wasn't.

I look at my journal entries from that season of my life, and the few that I found time to write are scattered, desperate prayers and frustrated ravings in which I blamed Scot, questioned God, felt totally lost and overwhelmed. I had no time or energy to write, to pray, to read—things that had previously been as normal a part of my day as eating and sleeping. I had believed that God was trustworthy, but now I was having trouble trusting him.

When I did, on occasion, read my Bible, I'd come across verses like James 1:2-3: "Consider it pure joy, my brothers, whenever you face trials of many kinds, because you know that the testing of your faith develops perseverance." My first thought was, *Yeah, right.*

When my kids would cry, often both at the same time, I'd feel overwhelmed, often to the point where I would look at them in frustration and cry myself. "Stop crying! Stop crying!" Of course, at the sight of my tears they would wail even louder. So the three of us would sit there crying for a few minutes, until my poor daughter would say, "Mommy, don't cry." I felt like a terrible mother.

In *The Problem of Pain* C. S. Lewis writes that "God whispers to us in our pleasures, speaks in our conscience, but shouts in our pains: it is his megaphone to rouse a deaf world."

At first I didn't hear him shouting. Frankly, I wasn't really listening. I was too busy shouting myself: "Why is this happening to me? Where are you?"

But God was there. And I was able to experience his presence in small ways—when I would just listen for a moment. God was present: in the peaceful face of my son as I nursed him, in the wise words of the Christian counselor who helped me work through the anger and sadness, in the cups of coffee shared with my best friend, who had given birth to her second child just three months before I had and understood some of what I was going through, at least on the parenting side of things.

And sometimes God was there in a calming presence that just said, "I love you and I understand. No matter what you go through, I will never leave you. I will take care of you." And the verse in James was true. Trials did produce perseverance. I kept going. And as I went, I kept finding God faithful and trustworthy.

Handing Over Your Wallet

To pray "Give us this day our daily bread" suddenly takes on new meaning when the sole breadwinner is not winning any bread. But the situation allowed us to see how generous God can be. Earning money through our work creates an illusion that we are in control; that it is our sweat or smarts that provides for our needs, rather than God's generosity. And while we need to play our part, everything we have is from God. I could not see this until we were forced to rely entirely on God.

When my husband lost his job, he received a severance package that gave him his regular pay for fourteen weeks. Also, he could collect unemployment even while receiving his severance pay, which allowed us to receive a small additional check from the state each week. So after he was laid off, our income actually went up for a while, even though the only work Scot was doing was sending out résumés and interviewing. Oh yes, and dealing with a newborn baby, a slightly jealous two year old and a manic, postpartum wife! But the fact that he was still getting paid was somewhat reassuring.

There were other tangible signs of God's care. The week after Scot was laid off, we received five different checks in the mail, all of them unexpected dividends from investments or payments for writing projects I had done a few months earlier. Despite my sad, overwhelmed feelings I felt like God was reaffirming in a tangible way that he would meet our needs. He was also reminding me that he was in control. It was getting me ready for when the severance package and the unemployment ran out, and we started tapping into savings. But Scot started selling houses before the savings ran out, and although the income wasn't regular, at least it was there again.

Being at home, where I am working but unpaid, is frightening for me, whether Scot is employed or not. Although I sometimes generate income with freelance writing jobs, I have had to learn to be financially dependent on my husband. When Scot lost his job, I couldn't go back to work. Who would hire a woman who looked like she had stopped off at the job interview on her way to the labor and delivery room?

Hearing God's whisper requires trust. We have to believe that what he tells us is true. Often that trust is developed through testing. Unemployment is a great test of trust.

Because really, if I don't trust God, the whole idea of living in his presence is silly. Why would I want to connect intimately with someone I don't trust? Why would I want his direction and input? For trust to grow, it must be tested. Otherwise, it's just theory, just hypothesis. That God is faithful must be proven, and it is often proven in the chaos.

God Heals the Floppy Disk

While I was writing this book, I had a little computer glitch. I went to pull up my manuscript, and I got a scary little box on my computer screen telling me I had "irreparable disk damage." I prayed over the disk; I cursed the disk. I tried three or four times to pull up the file, to no avail. I tried talking at the computer: "Come on! What's the matter?"

I went running the next morning and prayed as I jogged, "Lord, why is this happening? I thought you wanted me to write this book, and now you want me to retype it?"

As I jogged, the thought came, as if God were chuckling, "Just giving you another chapter!" I stopped in my tracks. I was writing about trusting God, but I didn't trust him with this very book. God seemed to be saying, "Quit complaining and pray with faith. Then just trust me."

I invited a computer-whiz friend over for a floppy-disk house call. We went to pull up the file, and amazingly, there was the entire manuscript. I quickly saved it to the hard drive and another backup disk, thanked my friend, who really hadn't done anything, and thanked God for rescuing my computer file. I still don't know how this happened. I attribute both the problem and the solution to divine intervention: an annoyingly concrete object lesson in trusting God not just with the huge crises like unemployment but with all the little details of my life.

I Am with You

It is one thing to say you trust God. It is another to have to trust him because everything else you were relying on has disappeared. When trust becomes more than theoretical, it grows. I did not want to be at home with two babies and an unemployed husband, but that is exactly where God wanted me.

At first I thought, *I'm going through this trial so that someday I will look back and see its purpose.* But that is not it . . . exactly. I was going through this trial because God had some things to teach me right then. I wasn't going to figure them out when the trial was over. I had to learn them in the moment, at the time: God is trustworthy; he is in control, not me. These were things I said I knew before this happened. But I didn't live as if they were true. That began to change when I had no other choice but to rely on him.

Looking back I see that I needed to enroll in this graduate-level course in trust. I needed to realize my dependence on God not only vocationally and financially but also in my role as a mother.

Until my son was born, I had considered myself (not very humbly) a pretty great parent. My daughter was precocious. She walked early, talked early and learned her ABCs early. I took much of the credit. After all, I had read most of the parenting books my local library had to offer and done a pretty terrific job of applying their principles to the upbringing of my daughter, or so I thought. I read to her daily from the time she was two weeks old. I had worked at home two days a week; I had the career-motherhood balance thing nailed. I was supermom.

Ha!

Just before Scot was laid off, I felt like God was telling me to take some time to focus on motherhood and ministering to my children. *Okay God, I'll trust you,* I thought. I started saying no to freelance jobs about halfway through my pregnancy. With careful budgeting we could make it on one income. I could do this. My kids needed me. God would take care of us.

Wham!

In the chaotic first year of my son's life I had to let go of my attempts to be a perfect parent. At times I was a pretty pathetic mother. But admitting that was the first step to becoming a better parent. Because instead of beating myself up for being imperfect, I began to pray. They weren't very pretty prayers at first, but at least I prayed. And I sought help: from other parents, from a counselor, from anyone I thought God might use to give me guidance.

"God, I need you here," I'd pray. "I can't do this alone." He was the knot at the end of my rope.

In the chaos God doesn't whisper, "I will take away your pain," and he doesn't say, "I will make everything smooth and easy." He only promises to be with you.

As I write this two years down the road, I'm amazed. God has blessed Scot's efforts in his new career so much. He has become one of the top sales agents in his office and is so busy that I rarely see him. Of course, that's another issue we're dealing with, just to prove that no one lives "happily ever after," until heaven. But in that time of testing God never abandoned us. He took care of us physically, emotionally and spiritually.

Today I see the fruit of the trials we went through. My ability to trust God is much greater. When Scot has a tough month and doesn't sell many houses, I trust God will bring another customer his way. And God does. When we found out that our car needed a new engine to the tune of several thousand dollars, I was able to trust that God would provide the funds. He did. When I'm ready to resign as a mother, he provides just a little bit of insight to help me be more loving toward my kids and toward myself.

He is faithful, and when I believe that enough to trust him, I feel his presence more concretely. But to go deeper into his presence I need to practice listening. For me, learning to listen was the next step in the journey.

For Reflection

1. Think of a time when a difficult circumstance forced you to rely on God. What made it hard to trust? Did God show his faithfulness to you? If so, how? What did you learn about yourself, and about God, as a result?

2. Do you worry about your finances? How does your worry make you act? Do you pressure yourself or your spouse to earn more money? (Ask your spouse for an honest appraisal on this.) Describe a time when you saw God provide for your physical needs.

3. Have the people closest to you (parents, spouse, best friends) been generally trustworthy? How do you think this might affect your ability to trust God?

4. What specific steps are you taking with your children that will teach them to trust their heavenly Father?

4

Developing a
Listening Heart

As I prepare dinner, the microwave whirs, then beeps. My daughter, in the late-afternoon crab zone, wails, "I want something to eat!" The baby has a diaper that needs to be changed, and as I lug him upstairs, my daughter's moans crescendo to a screech. "No, you can't have something to eat right now!" I yell, losing it. "Can't you just wait two minutes? We're going to have dinner as soon as I change this diaper!"

Melanie runs to her room, crying. My son whimpers. The phone rings, but I let the machine get it. The caller hangs up. The dial tone, then the beep of the machine echo in the kitchen.

In a world with so much noise I don't always know what to listen to. But I am learning that developing a listening heart requires that I stop listening to certain things: stop listening to television or the radio as "background noise." Stop listening to what advertisers and my peers tell me I need to have, need to hear, need to know.

The paradox of developing a listening heart is that it requires silence. Think about it. If my kids are peppering me with questions and won't stop talking enough for me to answer, I often have to begin with "Shhh! Listen." As I try to hear God's whisper, I sense him saying, "Shhh! Listen."

I began to spend time in silence. When the children were small and both napped, I would sit on the couch and try to do nothing except be still and silent. Instead of watching television or reading a magazine or even praying a monologue of requests for God, I would try to quiet down and listen to his side of the conversation.

At night, instead of flopping in front of the television for an hour or more, I would use the time after the children went to bed to clean up the kitchen in meditative silence.

Moms don't have much silent time. I thought I longed for quiet. But I found I had gotten so used to noise that I felt very uncomfortable at first without it. I was the first to complain about the racket, but I feared the emptiness of silence. But as I persisted in visiting a place of silence, it became more comfortable for me to go there.

"Though silence sometimes involves the absence of speech, it always involves the act of listening," Richard Foster writes in *Celebration of Discipline*. "Simply to refrain from talking, without a heart listening to God, is not silence."

Silence is an island in the sea of noise. Like it or not, we have to go there to hear the whisper of God. If we are to hear God's voice, we must first shhh, then listen. Not only to him but to his creatures.

Practice Listening to People

In his classic book on Christian community, *Life Together,* Dietrich Bonhoeffer writes, "The first service that one owes to others in the fellowship consists in listening to them. Just as love to God begins with listening to his Word, so the beginning of love for the brethren is learning to listen to them. It is God's love for us that he not only gives us his Word but also lends us his ear. So it is his work that we do for our brother when we learn to listen to him."

James 1:19 exhorts us to "be quick to listen, slow to speak and slow to become angry." Of course, when we do the first two, the third is likely to become much easier.

What does it mean to be "quick to listen"? When I converse with others, do I really try to listen and understand them, or do I simply use the time they are blabbing on to think about what I will say next? Do I hear only one part of what they say and then zone out so I can compose a sermon of advice on that part while they finish talking?

As I began to get intentional about listening to God, I began trying to listen to people. When I found myself in adult conversation (a rarity I ought to appreciate a bit more than I do), I actually listened in attentive silence. As a result, I found a new perspective on the relative unimportance of my words in relation to what someone else had to say, or what God had to say to me through them. It was remarkable. I wondered, what if I tried really listening to others—say, my husband—in this way?

Active listening begins with the ability to engage emotionally without speaking. To communicate care and attention through our expression and body language more than our advice giving is not easy. But the more I listen, the better developed my listening skills become. If I become good at listening to people, I can begin to better listen to God. I can become a listener.

How can I do this? It begins with the basics: closing my mouth. The discipline of silence is one I can practice both in solitude and with other people. As the Bible says, be slow to speak. But that is not enough.

It also says, be "quick to listen." I think that means being attentive, not just to stop talking but to engage fully in listening. The next time you have a conversation, try paying attention. Really paying attention with your whole self. Face the person. Look into their eyes. Don't interrupt. Don't allow yourself to zone out or think about what wisdom you will bestow on them.

The simple technique of "reflecting" what a person says by repeating or paraphrasing it transforms conversations. We become better listeners, and those we speak with open up more willingly. As they share more of themselves, we learn about them and from them. We also minister to them. We move toward God and bring them along with us.

Approach conversation gently, as an opportunity to learn

about someone else, to allow God to touch you through that person. Mirror back what you've been told by using phrases like "I hear you saying . . ." Draw someone out by asking, "What happened next?" instead of jumping in to offer unsolicited advice.

When I first began to make these simple efforts, they felt a bit awkward. But I found that if I persisted, I was rewarded not only with better listening skills but closer friendships. When I practiced this gentle listening, I not only extended grace to someone else, I often unexpectedly found my own soul nourished.

Listening like this will, not surprisingly, encourage the person to speak, perhaps to tell you more than you expect or desire to know. It will test your patience. Don't be afraid when the other person bares more of her soul than modesty suggests she ought. Accept that. Tell yourself, and tell her, it's okay. Feelings, and the discussion of feelings, are valid. Your ability to hear this person without judgment will allow both of you to hear God's whisper more clearly.

Listening to God

As I thought about developing a listening heart, I realized that to do so I would have to table my own agenda. That's hard. If you are at home all day with little children, you become hungry for conversation with someone other than your kids. Focusing on their needs makes you long for someone to focus on yours. If you work outside the home, you may feel exhausted from juggling the needs of your clients, your boss and your coworkers all day, and then com-ing home to a needy family. You don't have time to listen to anyone else. But a listening heart focuses on another, whether that other is a child, a friend, a client or God himself. When we focus on another, God speaks to us.

There's many times when my kids will be talking and talking and talking and I'll say, "uh huh, uh huh." And then my daughter will stop and say, "Mom! You're not listening!" Unfortunately, sometimes she's right.

God most often speaks to us through people. Of course, he uses other methods to communicate as well. Sometimes he uses the Bible to speak to us: a verse seems to jump off the page because it applies so directly to our situation. He also uses inner promptings or leadings that we may feel intuitively: we know what is morally right, or what we ought to do, and his Spirit seems to push on our soul to make the right choice. Sometimes he uses the natural world to remind us of his creative power: a spectacular sunset, a rainbow, a waterfall, a mountain.

But most often he uses the people around us to guide us and teach us. So I need to pay attention to what others tell me. Who do you spend most of your time with? Your kids? Your boss and coworkers?

God uses people of all ages and walks of life to communicate with us. God is always talking to me through my kids, since that is who I spend most of my time with. His favorite topic when using them: trust.

When Melanie was about eighteen months old and I was pregnant with Aaron, we flew to California to visit my parents for Thanksgiving. I used a frequent flier ticket for my daughter and myself. If she sat on my lap, or what was left of my lap by that point in the pregnancy, she could fly for free. However, the cost of a regular ticket for my husband on that airline was nearly double the fare we found on another airline. So my husband was on one plane, while Melanie and I were on another. The trip to California was long but relatively uneventful.

But on the way home the pilot informed us that we would have to fly through and around a series of snowstorms. Hearing this, I told Melanie, "We need to pray for Daddy and that we all get home safely," and we did, right in our seat on the plane.

The weather continued to worsen. The four-hour flight to Chicago slowly stretched into five, then six hours. After endless circling over Iowa, waiting for clearance into O'Hare Airport, we were forced to stop downstate in Peoria, Illinois, to refuel. There was talk of having to stay there overnight. But eventually we took off again for O'Hare.

When we finally landed in Chicago and I saw about a foot of snow on the taxiway, I felt frightened. Bad weather is not unusual in Chicago, and the airport crews usually clear snow much faster than the street plows do. But the runways were still buried, and the snow was still falling. We had friends picking us up, but I didn't know if they were there. I didn't know when Scot's flight, which had originally been due in about one hour after mine, was actually going to arrive. For all I knew, my friends could be stranded on the tollway, and Scot's plane could be parked on a runway in Peoria or Des Moines.

"Oh, Melanie, what are we going to do about picking up Daddy?" I said, more to myself than to her.

"Pray," she replied, her blue eyes looking straight into mine. Before I could respond to this pearl of wisdom, she waved her arms like a preacher and elaborated loudly, "Amen, Mommy! Amen, Daddy! Amen, Melanie!"

People around us on the plane smiled. I almost cried, reminded by my little girl of God's faithfulness. As it turned out, we had to wait for Scot for a while, but we all made it home safely. And we've never taken separate flights since!

As I have worked to cultivate my ability to listen, I have found that my relationship with God is greatly influenced not only by *who* but also by *what* I choose to listen to. When I feel like I can't sit down to pray because little ones would be climbing into my lap, I can put on a worship music tape. Then I can turn the distraction into a chance to cuddle my kids and sing to them about Jesus.

If I choose to make the effort to go to church and listen to godly teachers reveal truth to me, it is easier to converse with God the next day than if I had chosen to do something other than go to church. But I need to be careful here: too often when I'm listening in church, I'm thinking, *So-and-so ought to be here to hear this,* instead of worrying about the ever-growing log in my own eye! Thinking about what others could learn if they went to church, instead of focusing on what I should learn, is a type of pride that is a far greater sin than sporadic church attendance. What I need to be concerned with is what God is saying to me, not what he could say to someone else if they were here!

Sometimes who or what I listen to can influence my behavior and my connection with God in a negative way. If I am standing around the playground with some other moms, and they begin to gossip about someone who is not there, I feel uncomfortable. That's because I face a choice: join in, stand there and listen, or walk away. Although the second choice, to listen but not say anything, seems like a "better" choice, it really is not. Unfortunately it's the one I often make. I don't want to slander anyone, but I don't want to confront the gossipmongers and risk becoming the topic of their next session. Yet if I stay and listen to their negative discussion, my connection with God is certainly not enhanced!

As I work to develop a listening heart, I see that God has a lot to say to me. He's gentle and good and powerful. I knew, because he had brought me through some trials, that he was faithful. I am learning to listen to him. But sometimes there are internal issues that block my ability to hear him. The next step in my journey was to begin to work on those issues, the biggest of which is guilt.

For Reflection

1. What is drowning out God's still, small voice in your life? Describe a time when you felt highly connected to God.

2. Think of a time when someone really listened to you and stayed focused on you. How did you feel? Use this type of active listening in a conversation with a friend this week. What happens? How do you feel about it? Use the information you glean from this conversation to begin an ongoing conversation with God in order to pray for this friend.

3. What are some things that you listen to that are negative influ-

ences on your soul?

4. Do you think it is possible to follow the Bible's directive "Whatever is true, whatever is noble, whatever is right, whatever is pure, whatever is lovely, whatever is admirable—if anything is excellent or praiseworthy—think about such things" (Phil 4:8)? Why or why not?

5

. . . . .

Letting Go
of Guilt

My friend Lynn and I sat on the couch in the family room, trying to enjoy a conversation and a cup of coffee while our boys, ages fifteen months and eighteen months, buzzed around us like fighter jets: dip, roll, crash, recover . . . prepare for takeoff again. My three-year-old daughter was also on the floor, trying to build an elaborate block castle. Every five minutes one of the boys would make an emergency landing in the middle of a tower, and she'd shriek: "Mom! They're wrecking my stuff!"

Lynn and I would interrupt about every other sentence of our conversation with "Be careful!" and "Slow down!" and "Don't touch that!" We didn't know whether to laugh or cry over our attempt to talk to each other while refereeing squabbles and trying to keep the boys from spilling our coffee.

"Do you have quiet times?" she asked in confessional tone. "I mean, from the time he gets up until he goes to sleep, I don't have a minute to myself."

Lynn wasn't the first to ask. I had felt the same pangs of guilt. I considered a day a success if I found time alone for a shower, never mind a time of prayer and Bible study. How is it that I can find plenty of time to beat myself up for not spending enough time with God, but I can't find five minutes to just converse with him? But that is changing. I'm learning about living in his gentle presence and in his unlimited grace.

Guilt is a very unproductive emotion. It's real, but feeling it doesn't get us anywhere. It doesn't inspire action but rather more guilt. God, despite the unspoken messages of many of our childhoods, is not in the "guilty" business. In fact, his central message is "not guilty: forgiven."

You might be nodding, giving your intellectual assent. But how—emotionally, spiritually—do we move forward in our journey when guilt puts up roadblocks? Before we can live in God's presence, we need to tear down the soundproof wall of guilt that keeps us from hearing his voice.

I believe most Christians feel varying degrees of guilt about their spiritual lives. How much is enough? How much prayer time, how much Bible study, how many hours of stuffing envelopes in the church office? We are perfectly willing, most of us, to come to faith "just as I am" and to accept salvation by God's grace alone. Why then do we think that once we are adopted into his family, the rules somehow change and we are obligated to maintain our status? The actions that should be simply our grateful response to grace are twisted into rules we must keep to remain within God's favor. This confusion results in legalism and spiritual atrophy.

Brennan Manning puts it this way: "Our huffing and puffing to impress God, our scrambling for brownie points, our thrashing about trying to fix ourselves while hiding our pettiness and wallowing in guilt are nauseating to God and are a flat denial of the gospel of grace" *(The Ragamuffin Gospel)*.

I worry that I do not pray enough or correctly, or that I am not giving God enough of my time and energy. This type of thinking has never reduced the chaos in my life or strengthened my connection with him. Rather, it has put distance between us. Laden with guilt, I imagine God sitting in the corner where I usually pray, looking at his watch and wondering why I don't have time to sit and pour over Scripture and praise him for hours. But this, I am learning, is faulty thinking.

Setting New Benchmarks

When a company wants to see how it's doing against its competitors, it will benchmark other companies, comparing certain areas: productivity, employee benefits, quality management and so on. By benchmarking, the company can measure its progress, where it is doing well and where it needs a plan for improvements.

As a mother I get mired in guilt and frustration if I use the wrong benchmarks when it comes to spiritual growth.

In the church culture I grew up in and also the Christian college I later attended, the way people measured whether you were growing or not was with two key benchmarks: Did you have a daily "quiet time," and did you read your Bible? When someone asked, "So how's your walk these days?" they weren't wondering about your ability to propel yourself by moving your legs. They were wondering whether you were following the spiritual rules. Did you pray the right way this and every morning? Did you read your Bible? Whether or not you applied what you read there didn't necessarily seem to be as important.

Beyond that, there were other benchmarks that determined whether you were a Christian: Did you smoke, drink, gamble? If you did, your claim to be a Christian was certainly suspect. And you certainly couldn't be growing.

Bible study and prayer are good things. Drinking, smoking and gambling are not good things. But none of these are the benchmarks we should be using to determine whether or not we are growing.

 What, then, should the question be? Are we changing? Are we becoming more like Jesus or less like him? Are we becoming more patient, more kind, more loving, more gentle?

Most moms I know feel guilty about everything from daycare to disposable diapers. Christian moms don't always stand out in a crowd by their transformed lives. They are simply head and shoulders above other moms in the guilt department.

Along with the normal things to worry about (from breast-versus bottle-feeding to potty training and temper tantrums), they are also worried about how their spiritual lives seem to be slipping because they don't have a minute to themselves. And whether they are being "godly" parents. And whether their kids will grow up to know Christ or reject him.

This is not about being a supermom. I am hoping that now that we have reached the twenty-first century, we are well along into the postsupermom era, when we realize we can't do it all and have it all. We don't even necessarily want it "all."

What I want is not to be able to do it all but to have a new perspective on all I do, to let the work of mothering and all the other jobs that I do contribute toward my spiritual growth.

Learning from Your Mistakes

The kids and I are sitting down to dinner. "I'll pray," my daughter announces. "Dear Jesus, thank you for the food, and thank . . ." From her little brother come little puppylike noises, "Nnnn . . . Nnnn . . . Nnnn . . ."

"Aaron! Now I have to start over," she says in a very annoyed tone. "Dear Jesus, thank you for the food and for Mommy . . ."

"Nnnnn . . . Nnnnnn . . ." Aaron chimes in again. I squeeze his hand, but it doesn't quiet him. Melanie begins again.

"Dear Jesus, thank you . . ."

"I'm peeking," Aaron announces, opening his eyes and grinning at me. I shake my head and sigh.

"Aaron!" my daughter yells, exasperated.

"Melanie, don't start over. Just keep going and ignore him," I tell her.

"I can't. Dear Jesus . . ."

"Mmmmmmm," says Aaron.

"Aaugh!" cries Melanie.

"Stop it, both of you. Be quiet and I'll pray," I command, and I bark out, "Lord, thank you for the food. Amen."

Okay, I think, angrily hacking the kids' fish sticks into tiny pieces, *what exactly did I just teach my children?* Through my impatience, did I just destroy any possibility for a meaningful time of shared prayer? Or did that possibility only exist in my imagination?

As you can see, I have far to go as a parent. I blow it a lot. But what would you have done in the same situation? This is just one example of the type of situations I face on a daily basis, and just one of the ways guilt allows me to blow the significance of the situation way out of proportion. But God forgives. If I am clutching at guilt, I can't take hold of that forgiveness.

When my children make mistakes, sometimes I get impatient, but I try to comfort them with forgiveness. Why then is it so hard for me to accept God's forgiveness of my shortcomings?

There is a reason why Jesus taught us to call God "Father." He was trying to give us a clearer picture of what God is really like. He wants to comfort, to show his love, to accept us in spite of our mistakes. When I let go of guilt, I can receive his comfort with open arms.

Is This a Growing Season?

Spiritual growth and transformation are possible even during the years you are parenting preschoolers. In fact, these years, which I am still experiencing in all of their messy fullness, can be agonizingly difficult but amazingly fruitful spiritually. We just need some new benchmarks.

A great set of benchmarks are the fruit of the Spirit listed in Galatians 5:22-23: love, joy, peace, patience, kindness, goodness, faithfulness, gentleness and self-control. How are you doing on those? Are you allowing God to use the circumstances of your life to make you a more loving and gentler person? We can't become more joyful by powering up and trying really hard to be joyful. We have to be attentive for opportunities to feel and express joy, to laugh instead of scold when our kids are just being silly, to choose forgiveness rather than resentment with our coworkers or our spouse.

When we can shift our paradigm and let go of feeling guilty that we didn't get up before our kids at 5 a.m. to read and pray, we can allow God to use our circumstances to change us and make us more like him. That's not to say that we shouldn't find some time for solitude and prayer (more on that in a later chapter), but we should begin to let go of guilt about it. Instead of benchmarking with solitude and prayer, try seeing how you're doing on the discipline of service and perseverance through daily trials like getting meals on the table.

When you are trying to make dinner and your toddler is playing the percussion part of the *1812 Overture* on your pots and pans, and your three year old is hanging on your leg whining, "I'm hunnnngrrreeeeeeeee!" it's annoying as anything, but it can be an incredible opportunity to develop patience. Unfortunately, we can't develop patience unless we live in places that might make us lose it once in a while.

Time alone with God can help us grow, but so can serving others. Instead of feeling guilty about how little time alone I get, I need to look at how I can connect with God in the midst of my chaos.

I spend most of my day serving two little cute but very needy people. I have opportunities galore to practice patience and gentleness when they spill, dawdle, forget, spill . . . I have opportunities to show my love in tangible actions like making peanut butter and jelly sandwiches or kissing boo-boos. These moments "count" for spiritual growth.

We tend to think that only deep quiet contemplation or perhaps serving on a mission trip or volunteering in the church office "counts" in God's eyes. Nothing could be further from the truth, and nothing could be more defeating to a mother who finds that taking care of her children feels like almost all she can do.

This is the good news for mothers: the grungy, seemingly insignificant serving you do—cleaning up messes, wiping noses (and other body parts), preparing meals, dressing, un-dressing and bathing your kids—all of these things count in God's eyes. You are engaging fully in the discipline of service. If you can begin to view it as such, every little part of your day can be a way to connect with God.

And all the parts of mothering that you love, like the way they fly into your arms when you get home from work or cud-dling with a bedtime story or drying their tears, those count too. They please the heart of God.

And God is not deducting points on some giant tally sheet

in heaven because you missed your "quiet time." He's watching the way you trim the crust off the peanut butter and jelly sandwich and cut it in triangles because that's how your toddler likes it, and he's saying, "Well done, good and faithful servant."

When I let go of guilt, I can hear his whisper more clearly. But my life remains cluttered. If I want more room for God, I realize I am going to have to do some serious thinking about getting rid of some of the stuff in my life that crowds him out.

For Reflection

1. What three things do you feel most guilty about as a parent? Why?

2. What benchmarks of spiritual growth did you grow up with? What new benchmarks would you like to use?

3. Do you agree or disagree that your years of parenting young children can be fruitful spiritually? Why or why not?

6

. . . . .

Keeping
It Simple

ello, Mrs. Kent? It's Jackie from AMVETS. We're going to be in your area next week and wondered if you had anything you'd like to donate?"

"Sure, I can find a few things," I reply. About every two months Jackie calls. More often than not, I manage to scrape together a bag or two of clothes, toys, whatever, to give to charity. It's a good incentive for closet cleaning, and you get a tax deduction.

But this time, as the pickup date drew nearer I put a large box in the front hall and began cleaning closets in earnest. I had a strong urge to put everything in the box. But that desire wrestled with another that wanted to keep everything just in case I might need it someday.

Why is it that I can let go of a few things every two months? Why couldn't I put the things that are in the box in the front hall this month into the box two months ago? It's as if I'm prying loose, one clenched finger at a time, the tight fist with which I hold my possessions. What keeps me from opening my hands?

I am learning that if I want to live in God's presence, I need to get rid of nonessentials. I feel a strong desire to simplify. But what exactly does that mean?

Does it mean getting rid of more clothes and toys? Maybe it means not buying any new ones for a while. Would simplifying reduce the chaos in my life, enabling me to draw closer to God?

Oversimplified Simplifying

The antidote for chaos is simplicity. Whether you are studying quantum mechanics or arranging flowers, this is true.

I find it interesting: during the last one hundred years our lives have become infinitely more complex, but the latest lifestyle trend is that of "downshifting" or "simplifying." Yuppies who embraced conspicuous consumption and said "greed is good" during the upwardly mobile 1980s now sail a different tack. Lately it seems that everyone from interior design experts to corporate downsizers is telling us "less is more." Having too much stuff and spending too much time earning money to buy more stuff is part of what makes life chaotic.

There are hundreds of books, most of them aimed at former yuppies who want to jump off the fast track, offering advice on how to reduce spending, reduce clutter and get back to basics.

"When you stop to think about it, it's not surprising that so many of us want to simplify," writes former real estate investor turned simplicity author Elaine St. James in her book *Living the Simple Life*. "Never before in the history of mankind have so many people been able to have so much, go so many places, and do so many things. We've worn ourselves out trying to have it all. And now we're ready to look at other options."

Indeed, according to some estimates one in three Americans have downshifted their careers, cutting back on their hours at work or making other lifestyle changes in order to improve their quality of life, even if it means taking a pay cut.

There are a number of excellent books available on how we can simplify our homes, streamline our schedules, clean our closets and organize our lives. But I found myself hungry for something more than clutter reduction.

Simplicity of Another Kind

The traditional Christian discipline of simplicity goes far beyond eliminating possessions or cleaning closets, as Richard Foster so aptly describes in his book *Freedom of Simplicity*. He explores the paradoxes that make up what he calls "the complexity of simplicity."

> Simplicity is a grace because it is given to us by God. . . . Of course, we must not forget the other pole of our tension, for simplicity is also a discipline. . . . What we do does not give us simplicity, but it does put us in the place where we can receive

it. It sets our lives before God in such a way that he can work into us the grace of simplicity.

As I spent the week throwing extra stuff in the box in my front hall, I kept thinking: *I still have a lot of stuff. Does that mean I'm not really simplifying? How much stuff do I have to put in the box before I get to the place where I can receive the grace of simplicity?*

As I prayed and reflected on what simplicity means, I realized that it has more to do with contentment than with how many pairs of pants I own. My stuff was not the only thing in my way.

Paul wrote to the Philippians, "I know what it is to be in need, and I know what it is to have plenty. I have learned the secret of being content in any and every situation, whether well fed or hungry, whether living in plenty or in want. I can do everything through him who gives me strength" (Phil 4:12-13).

Truth about me is, I'm more content in plenty than in want.

But having been through the struggle and frustration of unemployment and the uncertainty of a career change, I knew that God was faithful in the times of want. So faithful, in fact, that we always had plenty, even in our time of want. And that, I think, is what Paul is saying. When we are focused on God first, we realize that we can be content because God will take care of our other needs, for food and shelter, for peace in times of trouble. He will give us courage not to throw away all of our possessions but to hold them with grateful and open hands.

"The Christian Discipline of simplicity is an inward reality that results in an outward life-style," wrote Richard Foster in *Celebration of Discipline* in 1978, decades before simplicity became trendy. "The inward reality of simplicity involves a life of joyful unconcern for possessions."

A joyful unconcern for possessions. I want to have that. But there are some possessions that are harder to let go of than others. I began to wonder about what motivates me to keep the stuff I do.

Trophies in the Closet

Half of the closet in my daughter's room is occupied by business clothes that I bought ten years ago and wore until I quit working in an office and began the adventure of motherhood. Despite the fact that these suits are tailored, classic styles, let's face it: they just look old. I don't wear them to church, and when I do freelance work, it's almost always over the phone, so I don't need them for that.

By the time I'll need business suits again—if ever—most of the ones in that closet definitely will be out of style. Most of them already are. I know the gray pinstripe one that I wore to my first job interview in 1985 is. That one's only of sentimental value.

But why all the others? Perhaps because I paid what seemed at the time like a lot for them or maybe because I don't want my entire wardrobe to consist of sweats and T-shirts, I keep them in the back of the closet.

They're like trophies, those pinstriped, dress-for-success suits. I don't wear them because people at the grocery store or the playground would look at me funny if I did. But once, when I was a full-time career woman, I wore them proudly. For me, my stuff is about pride. I want to show people my stuff, my suits. It is as if I want to tell people, I didn't always buy all my clothes at Target. I did important things and wore important clothes. I wore power suits, not drool-stained sweatshirts.

The stuff I hang on to, that clutters my physical world, creates spiritual barriers that keep me from hearing God's voice in the chaos. When I can let go of possessions that I really don't need and activities that keep me too busy, I can more readily find the quiet place within my soul.

A Single Eye

In *Freedom of Simplicity* Foster writes of having what the Bible calls a "single eye" or a singular focus on God that makes our lives simple because our connection with him is our top priority. Long before simplifying became something trendy for burned-out yuppies to embrace, heroes of the Christian faith were practicing it by embracing this concept of the "single eye." They weren't motivated by the desire for uncluttered closets—many of them didn't have closets or even more than one set of clothes. Instead, they were motivated by a single purpose: loving God.

Take, for example, John the Baptist. I'm not interested in following his dietary (locusts and honey) or fashion (camel's hair) recommendations, but he summed up the crux of Christian simplicity when he said this about Jesus, "He must become greater; I must become less" (Jn 3:30). As the King James Version puts it, "He must increase; I must decrease." I like that. As we get rid of our stuff and let go of the things with which we try to define ourselves, we decrease. But that's only half of it. Most yuppie simplifiers miss the other half: he must increase. What can I do to increase Christ's presence in my life?

Simplicity is, for me, about making room in my life for God to increase. And that's where the discipline part comes in. Disciplines such as prayer, silence and solitude.

God increases when I spend time with him: when I work hard to make the arrangements to have my husband or a friend or even a babysitter watch the kids for a morning, and use the time not to go buy more stuff or run errands but to walk through the forest preserve or sit in a quiet place and just be with God. It sounds extravagant, or maybe impossible, but really it is not. How is God going to increase when he's crowded out by the urgent demands of my work, my kids, my husband? How can I focus on God when everyone around me is jumping up and down waving his or her needs in front of my face?

What is simple to me is this: Jesus, lover of my soul. That's simple. That's where I want to focus. But I live in a cluttered house, both literally and figuratively. I have to cook, clean, pay bills and work. I have to invest emotional energy in my children, husband and friends. Certainly I receive as well as give relationally. But it makes life messy and chaotic. It does not feel simple most of the time.

But my life becomes more simple when I keep my focus, a single eye, on Jesus. When I'm caring for my family, I can focus on Jesus by knowing that what I do for them, I do for him, as we talked about in the previous chapter.

Simplicity is about slowing. To hear God's whisper, to live in his presence, I need to slow down. Not just put it in neutral for five minutes, with the motor revving, so that I can cross "quiet time" off my to-do list for the day. I need to take my foot off the gas and drive more slowly all the time. If I slow down my life and make it more deliberate, I can begin to live in Jesus' presence moment by moment. When I stop compartmentalizing my spiritual life, every facet of my existence can become spiritual.

Letting Go of "Ought To"

Despite the trend toward simplicity, I am still bombarded by messages that say I "ought to" have more stuff, better stuff, and that the stuff I have just won't do anymore and needs to be replaced.

On top of that, I feel pressure from any number of sources about what I "ought to" do: work more, volunteer more, read to my children more, keep house better and so on.

For me, simplifying is listening to God instead of the messages of our culture, and believing that it really is okay that I don't always keep my house spotlessly clean, or sometimes, even reasonably clean. It is okay that sometimes I don't always look or feel or act loving. It is okay that I'm not always patient with my kids. It is okay that I don't always have everything under control. My life is messy.

From that acceptance of myself, God's grace takes me to simplicity, a focus on him that puts all other things in proper perspective. When I let go of keeping impossible standards, I begin to live in God's presence.

But as I simplify, I realize this: I am spending most of my time with two little people who bring messes and complications into my life on a daily, even hourly, basis. They repeatedly test my ability to stay connected to God. How can I merge my parenting with my faith? What does God want to teach me in the midst of the chaos that my kids bring by merely existing?

For Reflection

1. Imagine that you are moving, and it's time to start packing. Look in your closets and drawers. Which items do you think are worth packing, moving and unpacking? Which items would you throw or give away?

If they aren't important enough to take with you, why do you still have them?

2. What can you do to simplify your schedule? While you can't give away a few of your "extra" children (as tempting as this might sometimes sound) or just up and quit your job (or could you?), some changes may be more feasible than you think. How many extra activities are you involved in?

How many hours are you working?

What can you eliminate?

3. "If all within us is honed down to the single treasure of Christ and his Kingdom, then we are living in the light of simplicity," writes Richard Foster in *Freedom of Simplicity*. Is Christ your "single treasure"? What other treasures, such as career, possessions, motherhood, education or popularity, compete to be your top priority?

4. Why would "focusing on Christ" simplify your life? What steps could you take to reorder your life to make Christ your primary focus?

7

.....

Experiencing God's Presence in Parenting

As the career chaos in my life waned, the family chaos waxed. Not only did I have two children less than two years apart, but as I mentioned earlier, my husband lost his job just before my son was born.

The particular brand of chaos created by children is complex: parents welcome the chaos children bring to their lives, yet long for a few moments of peace to escape it. At other times, being home with small children is boring. It feels like you're not really doing much, but you can't go do something else productive, either. For a recovering perfectionist and workaholic, this parenthood deal was a stretch.

When my daughter was born, I was still in the over-achievement mode. I was determined to be a great parent. During my pregnancy I had devoured child development books at about the same rate that I went through gallons of Edy's Grand Ice Cream. Once she was born, I kept a log of when I nursed her and for how long. Lest you think I am even more compulsive than I actually am, the main reason for this was that I was so sleep-deprived that I couldn't remember when I'd done anything! I was afraid I'd miss a feeding.

I should not have worried. My darling little baby had inherited my appetite, it seemed, and wanted to eat every two hours, often for almost an hour at a stretch. And like most babies, she was very good at making her needs known. One day I added up the hours on the log and realized just feeding this little chowhound was the equivalent of a part-time job! No wonder I considered the day a great success if I got the laundry folded. By the way, that's about the time I threw the nursing log in the trash!

I was totally amazed that one little person could take up my whole day. I remember once when my daughter was just a couple of months old, my husband walked in after work and looked around the house at the piles of laundry and unwashed dishes and said, "So, what did you do today?" I looked at him with tired resignation and pointed at Melanie, lying on a blanket on the floor, happily waving her arms and legs. It was the first time that day she hadn't been crying or eating, it seemed. "I kept her alive," I said. Never could I relate more to the Scripture "I am poured out like a drink offering" than those first few weeks of my kids' lives, when feeding, changing diapers and clothes repeatedly, more feeding and occasional naps made up my days and nights.

Life Lessons

Things didn't get simpler as my children got older (older meaning preschool age). They got a bit easier because I got more sleep, but they didn't feel simpler.

Before my children were born, I was (like most people who don't have children) clueless about raising them. I swore my children would not have any sort of formal lessons or schooling until they were five years old. I was sure their imaginations would bloom if they were unfettered by structured activities. But soon I began to rethink this strategy. The sheer length of Chicago winters and the challenges of finding creative indoor activities for a precocious and energetic preschooler overcame me. I allowed occasional park district classes and two mornings a week in the church nursery while I went to an exercise class at my church.

That was fine until my daughter started ballet class. Melanie seemed to enjoy it for several months, but suddenly, just before she turned four, she hit a phase where she developed an irrational fear of lessons of any kind. "I don't want to go!" she'd sob, "I just want to be with Mommy!"

If I hadn't been talking with God much before this, the situation certainly opened up my end of the conversation. "What should I do, Lord? She says she wants to do ballet, but when she gets to class, she just wants to leave." Was she manipulating me, or was she truly fearful? Should I allow her to quit? Should I force her to go? Sounded like a lose-lose proposition to me. If I let her just quit, I was sure she'd grow up to never be able to follow through on commitments. If I forced her against her will to continue, I envisioned her in therapy twenty years from now, talking about the psychological damage wreaked on her by a tyrannical mother.

Eventually I read some of David Elkind's books (*The Hurried Child* and *Miseducation: Preschoolers at Risk*) and decided to let her drop out of ballet. But I can't help thinking that if I had stuck to my original ideals on simplicity for my children, I would be spared the agonizing decision of whether to force her to attend lessons or not.

I have seen parents who sign their children up for three or four different lessons, so that they have some sort of activity going on almost every day. In my opinion, this kind of over-scheduling, especially in the preschool years, can be stressful. And if you work outside the home, then have to shuttle your kids to karate and tap dancing and chess club, your time with them is even more restricted.

Of course, being home all the time with your kids can also be stressful. I found a middle ground by signing up for "parent-tot" classes that I could do with my kids and avoiding highly structured classes like ballet. To give myself a break, I continued to attend the exercise class, and the kids seemed to like the loosely structured playtime with other kids in the church nursery. In my life these limits have reduced the chaos. My children meet other kids; I meet other moms; we get out of the house.

Also, I have found my kids enjoy outings with me even more than mom-and-tot classes. We go for walks through the nature preserve near our house or explore a new park in a different neighborhood. We visit the zoo or a children's museum or even the mall.

I wish I'd been wise enough to avoid ballet lessons. But I probably would not have learned some things about my daughter and about myself that I needed to learn. Sometimes the chaos is there for a reason, to stand in sharp contrast to the simple peace of God.

Simple Gifts

Though children add to the chaos, they also are experts at simplicity and at giving simple gifts.

As I mentioned earlier, my husband frequently works in the evenings, but his schedule also often allows him to be home in the morning. One morning he got up with the children, letting me sleep after a bit of a rough night, which started around 3 a.m. when Melanie had awakened from a nightmare and had climbed into bed beside me, her cold little feet against my legs jarring me from sleep. After a few moments of reassuring cuddling, I took her back to her own bed, and we all went back to sleep, but Aaron woke all of us again just before 7 a.m.

After a blissful hour and a half of sleeping in, I awoke when the bedroom door opened. In trooped my little family. Aaron proudly handed me a napkin and fork, Melanie gave me a glass of juice, and Scot handed me a plate of scrambled eggs, toast and apple slices.

"We made you breakfast, Mommy!" said Melanie, climbing in bed with me. "Can I have a bite?" We all sat on the king-sized bed, sharing bites of eggs and apples while the children told me all about how they had helped crack the eggs and butter the toast.

My husband and children told me nothing profound, nothing earth shattering. They did not share a theology lesson with me or even a Bible verse. Their gift was not perfect (there were a few shell bits in the eggs). Yet they showed me love that fed my soul. My husband demonstrated what a patient father and loving husband he is. My kids brought their typical exuberance. Theirs was a simple gift, a gift from God, and I accepted it with thanks.

Simple moments, simple gifts, find their way into my life when I have cleared away the unnecessary: the physical, emotional and spiritual clutter. If my life is too cluttered, the moments may come and go without my even noticing them. God will stand at the door and knock, but I'll be too distracted to even answer.

For Reflection

1. The next time you are watching your children at the playground, on the soccer field or as they play while you fold laundry, make it a time to connect with God. Pray for your kids with your eyes open, as you look at them. Thank God for them. Pray for his protection on them, today and for the rest of their lives. Pray for their spiritual development. Think about loving Jesus by loving your kids.

2. How many activities are your children involved in? If it's more than one or two, how could you simplify their lives?

If they are preschoolers, how do you think they would respond if you told them they didn't have to go to ballet, soccer or whatever?

How would you feel?

If you have older children, what might happen if you asked them to cut back to just one or two extracurricular activities?

3. Matthew 18:1-4 says, "At that time the disciples came to Jesus and asked, 'Who is the greatest in the kingdom of heaven?' He called a little child and had him stand among them. And he said: "I tell you the truth, unless you change and become like little children, you will never enter the kingdom of heaven. Therefore, whoever humbles himself like this child is the greatest in the kingdom of heaven." What does it mean to "become like little children"?

4. What admirable character traits do you see in your children? Describe their faith in you as a parent. Do you have a similar faith in God?

8

· · · · ·

Discovering
Simple Beauty

Once you have simplified by removing the unnecessary from your life, there is room to carefully arrange what remains in a way that will direct you toward God. For me, this was the next step in my journey toward deeper intimacy with God.

Whether you spend most of your time at home, in your car, at the office or a combination of all three, you can control your environment to some extent. You may work in a windowless cubicle, but you can put up pictures of your family, a piece of simple artwork or fresh flowers to make it less drab. You may live in a simple suburban tract house, a city apartment or a farmhouse, but you can find ways to make your home a place of beauty and order.

I am not a good housekeeper. Parents of young children walk in, look around and smile knowingly because of the toys cluttering the family room or the high probability on any given day of finding a tent or boat constructed of blankets and chairs in the dining room.

People who do not have children, on the other hand, walk in, look around and ask, "What happened?" There is always a fair amount of chaos in my house, in part because I live with two preschoolers and spend more time playing with them or, truth be told, sitting at my word processor than I ever spend cleaning!

As much as I value play, I also crave order. So I try to create little islands of orderliness among the clutter, and I work every day simplifying, trying to discard the unnecessary. I also have learned to ignore some of the chaos, to shut the door to the playroom and retreat to the couch upstairs or the backyard deck where I can sit for a moment and be still, read, write, look at the trees or simply pray for a moment.

Seeing Value in Beauty

I must confess that of all the chapters in this book, this one on beauty and order is the hardest for me to write. I am seeking God's wisdom and reading a lot on this subject. I know it is important, but to put it into practice is particularly challenging for me.

First of all, my tastes are quite simple, and I tend to be a bit of a tightwad. Because my job of mom and writer allows me to work at home, I need to dress for comfort and inevitable messes. I can satisfy most of my wardrobe needs at Target, where I can also pick up laundry detergent, diapers and shoes for the kids in the same trip.

It's hard for me to justify spending money on fancy French-milled soap just because it smells good when the discount store has Ivory on sale for $3 per twelve-bar economy pack. I own no fine china, instead choosing to set my everyday table with my mother's hand-me-down earth-toned pottery plates. When company comes, I pull out my plain white ceramic plates and put a tablecloth on instead of place mats, light the candles, and I'm set.

I tend not to bother with self-pampering that seems nonessential, but I am learning that if I don't take care of myself somehow, my soul will starve. So I am slowly changing my perspective, trying to find rituals and practices that feed my soul and nourish my relationship with God.

Second, as I said, I'm not a great housekeeper. What can I say? As I said at the beginning of this book, I'm writing not as an expert but as a fellow traveler.

When we are surrounded by piles of paper, dirty dishes and crumbs, we are, at best, distracted and, at worst, defeated. How often I start to pray, even as I go about my work at home, "God . . . I was thinking . . ." then suddenly I hear "Mommy!" from the other room, or the phone rings, or I look at the toys strewn all over the floor and I think, *Oh, I'd better pick those up.* My conversation with God, begun with the best intentions, is forgotten.

I have always longed to have a beautiful, well-ordered home. I want my home to be a haven. I have read enough books on this subject to know that I am not the only one who desires this and certainly not the only one who finds it a challenge. But how does an orderly and beautiful home help me live in God's presence?

God in the Details

Legendary architect Mies van der Rohe said, "God is in the details." Maybe so, but I am what I like to call a "big picture" thinker. I look at the grand scheme of things and often find details (like dusting) are a bother.

Although in some parts of my life, especially housekeeping, I like to skim over them, there is a benefit to paying attention to details. It is a discipline that forces me to live more deliberately. Making my home a place of beauty requires me to go a step beyond bulldozing the clutter off the tables and countertops into the drawers and closets. It means giving thought to creating a mood of peacefulness or comfort.

The discipline of paying attention to details at home is a training exercise for paying attention to the spiritual details of my life. In her book *Living a Beautiful Life* interior designer Alexandra Stoddard talks about small rituals, from meals to bathing to decorating, that can touch all of our senses, that can make our homes and our lives beautiful.

"You transform daily tasks into meaningful rituals by paying careful attention to the small details that go into those tasks," she writes. "Your senses can help you, can be your lightning rod, a guide to how you want to enliven your daily life."

Stoddard is not necessarily writing from a Christian perspective. She simply wants to make her life more pleasant, and she enjoys beauty. But God was the one who thought of beauty and created it in the first place. Making our environment beautiful, not ostentatious, can not only improve our appreciation for God's creation but boost our self-esteem. If we remember that, we can use rituals that improve the beauty of our life to remind us of God.

Slow Down and Sip the Coffee

Rituals that Stoddard and others write about force us to slow down. If we approach them correctly, as a means to growing spiritually rather than an end in themselves, they can help us to take control of some of the chaos that is inevitable in our lives.

For example, imagine the scene of breakfast at your home. Do you see children running everywhere, sack lunches and Pop Tarts flying through the air, you standing in your bathrobe in the middle of it trying to direct traffic as you gulp coffee from a chipped mug with your former employer's company logo on it?

Contrast this with Stoddard, who writes in her book that she cooks breakfast (I'm assuming she doesn't count "toasting" as cooking) and sometimes sets her breakfast table with "hand-painted Mustiere pottery from France."

There is such a thing as getting a bit extreme on the beauty and order thing, but if you did, say, put a place mat under your plate and scramble an egg, and sat rather than stood while you ate it, how would it affect your life and your connection with God? Would you feel a little less chaotic? Would it slow you down enough to perhaps thank God for the egg and for the fact that this meal is a little more satisfying than yesterday's, when you ate Toaster Strudel off a paper napkin and slurped lukewarm coffee from a travel mug as you drove for the carpool?

"Everything in our surroundings speaks for us, and if we accept living with a vulgar design we must pay for it. Caring about aesthetics increases your sensitivity. The more we care about the small details, the more in tune to beauty we become, and the more we realize how seemingly insignificant items affect us," Stoddard writes.

Stoddard is writing from a designer's perspective, but she knows how little details can make a big difference.

Is Beauty Breakable?

I am not talking about blowing your budget or spending huge amounts of time to decorate like Martha Stewart, nor am I espousing hedonistic focus on external pleasures. Beauty does not necessarily mean ornate, time-consuming or expensive.

When we visit some friends who don't have children, Melanie will often size up a living room full of knickknacks on low shelves with obvious trepidation, "They sure have a lot of breakables here, don't they?"

Beauty is not necessarily breakable. Often it is quite simple.

I have a number of pictures on the walls at my house. Most are photographs of my children. Someday I'll probably be one of those grandmothers who still has her kids' baby pictures up on the wall.

I also have an oil-and-pastel painting that I received as a barter payment for some writing work a few years ago. I would never have spent the money that the painting cost to buy it outright, but as a barter it seemed an opportunity I could afford. It is a beautiful piece of art, hung over the couch with a light shining on it to show the detail and color at its best.

Over my sink I have another work of art, done in multicolored crayon. It depicts a simple bouquet, with the words "Mother's Day" below. On a piece of lined writing paper glued on below the picture, the words "I love my mom because . . ." are printed. My dear friend Sue, a preschool teacher, had brought this "project" over when she watched my kids for me one evening. After both children colored the picture, she had taken this dictation from my daughter to complete the sentence "I love my mom because . . . she's my special friend." While the value and beauty of my Mother's Day card is something other people may not be able to appreciate, I think it is beautiful. The painting and the drawing both add beauty to my home, in different ways.

Beauty doesn't just come in things we can look at, and it need not be confined to the house.

My garden is as cluttered as my house. Gladiolus and cucumbers grow side by side with a few weeds. I tend to stick in the plants haphazardly as I find them at garden center sales, without any real plan. I call it a sort of modern art approach to garden design. It looks a lot like those paintings where the artist simply throws paint at the canvas. A riot of color, vines, vegetables and weeds. Despite the fact that my garden will never be featured in a magazine, it adds beauty and joy to my home—not only with the flowers that we cut but with the vegetables and herbs we harvest. When I look at a shelf crammed with canning jars full of homemade jam, preserves, pickles and other bounty from the garden, I can't help but marvel at God's generosity. The garden provides a picture of faith and of God's provision. From tiny seeds come baskets of food. From some time invested with the garden and with its harvest, I have a full pantry.

The sounds in your home can also add to its beauty. In our house, the television is off during the day, except for one or two videos for the kids. I never put on radio or television talk shows or soap operas or even public television while I'm working around the house, and I don't have a television in the kitchen or bedroom. We have one television with no cable or satellite. That gives us a choice of about six or seven stations, the newspaper or a good book. Some people choose to eliminate television altogether. My sports-fan husband and Barney-fan kids would never stand for that, but I try to limit its use. Because if I choose not to watch television, not only do I get rid of noise, but I also gain something: extra time for things that matter more.

If I choose to listen to soothing music or a worship tape, for example, my life feels less chaotic, even if my circumstances remain the same. When my kids are both whining and I'm feeling frazzled, there is nothing like music. Bach, Mozart or Mother Goose: sounds that distract the children at first, then soothe them.

There are such things as simple pleasures. Once I had begun the process of eliminating the nonessentials, I saw that I needed to fill in the spaces with beauty, things that brought me joy: a walk outside, flowers for the table, a photograph of our family, or a picture drawn by a friend or a child.

But getting rid of things and adding other things, isn't enough to usher me into God's presence. For that I am realizing that I need to do not just house cleaning but some soul cleaning. And that is accomplished in a rather lonely place.

For Reflection

1. Proverbs warns: "Better a meal of vegetables where there is love than a fattened calf with hatred" (15:17); "Better a dry crust with peace and quiet than a house full of feasting with strife" (17:1). What steps can you take, regardless of the physical appearance of your home, to bring love and peace into your home?

What would you change about the relational and emotional aspects of your home life?

2. Clear off your kitchen table or your desk at work and find something simple to set on it that will remind you of God (a seashell, a branch of a flowering tree, an autumn leaf, several colorful rocks in a glass of water). When you see this thing of beauty or simple truth, gently direct your thoughts toward God. Thank him for your relationship with him.

3. When you wash dishes, think about how Christ has washed away your sin. He has gently scrubbed the baked-on grime of your sin to make you brand new. Thank him as you wash each dish, that he has provided food for you and forgiven you of the messes in your life. If it helps you to focus, tape an index card with a favorite verse or quote on the wall above the sink.

9
· · · · ·

Connecting
Through Solitude

Much has been written about the need for us to care for our
souls. But we were not created to care for our own
souls exclusively. We were created to depend on
God and to nurture our souls through his Word, through his
Spirit, through his creation, both by reflecting on the beauty
of nature and by living in community with other people.

When I am still and quiet long enough to receive this nurture, I can hold it gently, then hand it to my children, my coworkers, my friends, even strangers. In this giving and taking
of love and community we live in God's presence. In my journey I found that making time for solitude was extremely difficult but essential if I was going to hear God's voice.

To work cooperatively with God to nurture my soul, to be able to hear his whisper, I must sometimes intentionally withdraw from the chaos.

Solitude and the closely related discipline of silence are shelters I can build to shield me from the storm that is my life. But to build these disciplines into my routine takes sacrifice and perhaps some discomfort. The benefits, like those provided by any shelter, are enormous.

As the mother of a toddler and a preschooler, the idea of solitude sounds wonderful. A day of silence, with absolutely no one crying "Mommmmy!" is my idea of bliss. I crave time alone, but am I willing to make it happen?

To let go of what feels like unavoidable obligations to spend even a couple of hours in solitude takes courage and an enormous amount of energy: finding a babysitter or friend to watch the kids, ignoring the piles of laundry on the floor and the cobwebs on the ceiling, and getting away. The effort required often stops me from even trying to have more than a few minutes during naptime for solitude and silence.

Maybe you think solitude would make you feel like a princess imprisoned in a tower, with nothing to think about except all the stuff you can't get done while you're just sitting there. But really, solitude is something we escape to, not from. For me, it requires that I slay the dragon of my imagined self-importance and escape the dungeon I've created with obligations.

If I can't get away for a whole morning or a day, I try to find even a few moments of solitude somewhere in my day. It is so difficult to be intentional about this. Often, instead of sitting in quiet solitude while the kids are napping or playing by themselves, I'll spend twenty minutes "straightening up." But it seems that things don't look that different when I'm done. I feel defeated.

When I am open to looking for opportunities for solitude, it's amazing how many God reveals. A morning walk before the kids are up, a half-hour with my Bible, my journal and a cup of coffee on the patio while the kids watch their morning video, a few moments in the afternoon while my son naps and my daughter plays alone. Of course, this last one tends to get interrupted by "Will you play Barbies with me?" or some similar request.

I often say I don't have time for solitude: I'd really like to be alone, but I'm too busy. I am, after all, the mother of two preschoolers. But the truth is, I avoid solitude because I fear loneliness. The paradox, if I can muster up the courage to explore it, is that solitude is actually an antidote for the poison of loneliness.

> Loneliness or clatter are not our only alternatives. We can cultivate an inner solitude and silence that sets us free from loneliness and fear. Loneliness is inner emptiness. Solitude is inner fulfillment. . . . Solitude is more a state of mind and heart than it is a place. There is a solitude of the heart that can be maintained at all times. Crowds, or the lack of them, have little to do with this inward attentiveness. (Richard Foster, *Celebration of Discipline*)

Solitude as Preventative Medicine

Solitude is a lot like exercise. Everyone wants the benefits of having engaged in it, but not everyone is willing to actually make time for it. We know it will be good for us. But to "just do it" is a struggle, even if we find the time. Like exercise, there are a million excuses for avoiding solitude. "I'm too busy." "I can't find anyone to watch my kids." "I'm an extrovert and just don't like to be alone." "I really would rather be serving God by volunteering my time with people." This last one wins lots of self-righteousness points.

Before I had children, I worked full-time as a newspaper reporter. Stress and deadlines were normal. I also volunteered my time at my church and had an active social life. Occasionally, when the pressure and busyness got to be too much, I'd call in sick, feigning some vague symptoms, rationalizing the deception by telling myself it was a "mental health day." I'd spend the day lounging around, maybe running errands, but usually just relaxing, catching up on sleep, reading, praying or writing letters.

Many of us approach solitude the same way. Solitude becomes something we seek out when we are on the brink of losing our mental stability, a sort of emotional disaster plan used in times of emergency.

I can avoid such meltdowns by planning solitude into my life as a sort of spiritual preventative medicine. It is hard. It is a discipline. But sometimes it is a gift to myself.

As I tried to hear God's whisper, I decided I needed to build solitude into my life. As the result of careful negotiations, my husband has our children one morning a week. He'll play with them at home or take them to his office and put them to work sticking address labels on flyers. I take that time to get out of the house and spend time alone. Sometimes I write. Other times I read my Bible. Sometimes I go for a walk.

But I try to spend part of that time each week just sitting quietly. I may read a short passage of Scripture to get my mind focused. I'll whisper a short prayer like "Come, Lord Jesus." Then I just wait. Sometimes no thoughts or insights come. Sometimes worries crowd into my mind. I gently turn them over to God and invite his presence again. Sometimes I get clear answers to my prayers. Other times I just feel God's presence in a sort of peacefulness and rest.

When you find yourself unexpectedly alone, don't rush to turn on the television or call a friend. And even if you are surrounded by people, cultivate a quiet spirit, an "inward attentiveness" to your own soul and to the leadings of God's spirit.

I am learning that if I want to have God's strength in the times of chaos, I will find it in quiet, peaceful moments with him. I am better equipped for the storms of life if I build a shelter of solitude.

When I go into that shelter, God can fill my emotional tank, replenish my spirit. I need time like that. Not time to read *Good Housekeeping* in the tub after the kids have gone to bed (although this can be quite therapeutic), but time where I pray, meditate on Scripture, and simply sit and listen.

Times of solitude help keep my focus on God during times when I am surrounded and overwhelmed by the cares and commitments of my life.

Following Jesus to the Lonely Place

If the idea of putting aside your obligations for an hour, a morning or even a whole day seems selfish, look to Jesus' example. Repeatedly the Gospels note that in the midst of busy days of teaching and healing, Jesus "withdrew to a lonely place and prayed there." I don't think he was being selfish. He knew what was important.

The life of Jesus ebbed and flowed between solitude and service. In Matthew 14 I read that John the Baptist was beheaded. Beginning with verse 12, it says that "John's disciples came and took his body and buried it. Then they went and told Jesus. When Jesus heard what had happened, he withdrew by boat privately to a solitary place. Hearing of this, the crowds followed him on foot from the towns."

Imagine yourself in Jesus' place. His cousin, the prophet who had proclaimed him, the man about whom Jesus had said, "Among those born of women there has not risen anyone greater than John the Baptist" (Mt 11:11) has just been senselessly killed. Jesus wants some time alone to grieve, to pray, to mourn the loss of this friend and coworker in the kingdom. But instead of getting solitude he gets needy crowds looking for a miracle or a touch.

When I'm longing for solitude, and the crowd of my two children comes following me to my solitary place, I get frustrated and sometimes even angry. I need some time alone, and I can't get it. But Jesus responds differently than I would. The very next verse says, "When Jesus landed and saw a large crowd, he had compassion on them and healed their sick." The next six verses describe the feeding of the five thousand. He goes beyond compassion to extend himself, to serve these people who seem insatiable in their hunger for him.

As the mother of young children I'm often tempted to give up on solitude or meditation. *I can't do those disciplines,* I think.

I'm like Jesus, always interrupted with other people's needs. He had to turn loaves and fishes into a feast for a crowd; I've got to turn leftovers into an edible dinner. Sometimes I feel like I need a miracle to make it happen.

So should I just give up on solitude because I am in a serving season of life? It is precisely because we can't typically go to the bathroom alone that we need times of intentional solitude. Times when we get someone else to watch our kids, draw a line in the sand and say, today, for an hour or two or even three, I'm going to be alone with God.

Alone.

Does it seem impossible?

The more it seems impossible, the more you need it.

If you keep reading in Matthew, you'll see that Jesus temporarily shelved his need for solitude, but he did not disregard it entirely.

After feeding the crowd, he sent the disciples on ahead in a boat. Then he set some firm boundaries. The Bible says he dismissed the crowd (14:22). He didn't say, "Leave if you like, stay if you want." He didn't say, "Why don't you stay all night and maybe I'll do a pancake miracle for breakfast." He knew the disciples needed a break, and so did he.

He made no apologies. "Immediately Jesus made the disciples get into the boat and go on ahead." He made them. He didn't suggest or ask. He made them. Immediately. End of discussion. The disciples, who had been longing to get away from the crowd since long before dinner, gladly climbed into the boat and set sail.

Then he dismissed the crowd. His dismissal apparently left

no room for discussion, since the Bible says in the same sentence that "he went up on a mountainside by himself to pray" (v. 23). He got the solitude he needed. He gave his disciples direction but then let them go on their own way for a while. He took the time that he now needed even more than before. Time to deal with his sadness over John's death. Time to reflect on what God had done through him. His time of solitude and prayer was not a luxury. It was a necessity. He was hungry for it the way the crowd had been hungry for dinner, hungry for his healing touch.

So he goes to the hills, his lonely place. A solitary retreat on a rugged hillside. There he meets God and finds rest. After so much pouring out, he lets God pour life and strength back into him. And it so rejuvenates and strengthens him that three verses later, he's walking on water!

When I am tempted to give up on my quest for solitude, I look at Jesus' example. When I think I will never have silence, I read these verses and ask myself what boundaries between service and solitude I need to draw.

There is a time for both. Through solitude we are strengthened for service. There's an ebb and flow. If you're not sure what the balance is, keep adding more solitude until it feels right. Solitude fuels service. You'll see that Jesus regularly withdrew into solitude and that it strengthened him so that he could return to serve people.

Jesus also uses solitude not just to recover from draining ministry experiences but also to prepare for key turning points in his life. Before he chooses his disciples, before his death, Jesus is described as withdrawing to a lonely place to pray. He knew that solitude fortified him, because it was there that he heard God's voice most clearly.

If I desire to be Christlike, to grow, I will do well to imitate the rhythm of solitude and service in Jesus' life. The more chaotic my life becomes, the more I need a "lonely place," a place of solitude that I can visit temporarily to gain perspective. Henri J. M. Nouwen examines this truth in his compelling little book of meditations *Out of Solitude.*

> To live a Christian life means to live in the world without being of it. It is in solitude that this inner freedom can grow. Jesus went to a lonely place to pray, that is, to grow in the awareness that all the power he had was given to him; that all the words he spoke came from his Father; and that all the works he did were not really his but the works of the One who had sent him. In the lonely place Jesus was made free to fail. . . . A life without a lonely place, that is, a life without a quiet center, easily becomes destructive.

In solitude there is freedom. When I move into solitude, I take control back from other people and give it to God. As Nouwen says, we escape destruction: destruction of our souls, destruction of peace—which is, essentially, chaos.

By engaging in solitude, by visiting a lonely place where we connect with God and ourselves, we say no, at least temporarily, to the demands of others. We say yes to God. In so doing we gain strength for dealing with those pressures when we return. We gain the strength to set boundaries, to say no to things that would pull us away from our purpose and from our soul's connection with God. If we are unsure what that purpose is, times of solitude will help us determine it.

Solitude is difficult because we must sacrifice our to-do list in order to make time for it. We must willfully decide that certain things will not get done, at least not immediately. The joyful paradox in making time for solitude is that it slows us down enough to help us realize which things on our list are actually worth doing, and we end up with more time to do the few things that truly matter.

For Reflection

1. What do you think are the benefits of solitude? What are the three biggest barriers in your life that keep you from spending time in solitude? What steps could you take to overcome those barriers?

2. Spend several hours in silence. Swap babysitting with a friend or use part of a day when your husband has the day off. Get your children out of the house or get yourself out of the house. No radio, no TV, no conversation (if possible). If you like, pray, but spend some of that prayer time just listening, paying attention to what God is impressing upon you. Take part of the time to read, to sit and think, or to just sit.

3. Spend ten minutes in the morning in silence and solitude. Set your alarm to awaken early, before your family rises or before you need to get ready for work. Focus on God and any of his blessings. Thank him specifically for five things in your life, such as health, relationships, the roof over your head or whatever comes to mind. As you move slowly into your day, try to cultivate the "inner attentiveness" that Foster talks about. At the end of the day spend ten minutes alone again. Jot down any observations about the experience in a journal. What is it like to begin and end a day with solitude? What would happen if you did this consistently?

10

.....

Hearing God's Calling

A s a mother, I am conflicted. It is the strangest job in the world, really. I find myself wondering one minute *How can I possibly do it all?* and the next thinking *Is this all there is?*

I have tried to simplify my life and to live in God's presence moment by moment. I have tried to develop a listening heart and to pay attention to what God is teaching me through trials, both the big ones and the everyday ones.

Still, as I go through my day, I feel busy and overwhelmed most of the time, and a bit bored and restless the rest of the time. Part of the problem is choices I make: choices to do too much, to please others, to ignore my own needs. But I also of-

ten fail to see my work as God's calling on my life. I sometimes feel I am just putting in time, trying to survive another
day.

Most of the people I know, whether married or single, at
home or divided between home and an office, feel they have
too much to do. They feel guilty because they don't have
enough "time for God." Unless they are working at a church
or other "ministry" full-time, they typically don't see their
day-to-day duties as a "calling."

For a long time much of my prayer time was spent throwing such questions at God, trying to get him to open up and
reveal the "grand purpose" for my life, to reveal to me my
"calling" so that I could get on to the important part of my
life. The age-old questions "Who am I?" and "Why am I
here?" and "What should I do with my life?" haunted me. But
as I learned to listen to God, I realized that my purpose may
not be as grand as I imagined. Quite possibly, it was rather
ordinary.

Yet ordinary, when embraced, becomes extraordinary.

It is possible that I am right where I am supposed to be for
now. Your calling might be to become a missionary to Africa,
but it is more likely not to be. Your calling may be to shine the
light of God's truth in a dark marketplace for a while, then to
raise children for a season, then to move on to a different career. Maybe those things will overlap at times. Or it may be to
be a missionary to the factory or office or shop where you
have found a job that you can do well.

Our calling is to carefully determine what God wants us to
do and then do it with all of our energy. We begin to deter-

mine it by looking at where we are now. Did we get there by making mistakes or by following God? If it is the latter, we have probably found what it is that God wants for us, at least for now. Your calling may include your roles as wife, mother, employee or friend.

Frederick Buechner writes in his collection of essays *The Hungering Dark*, "We can speak of a man's choosing his vocation, but perhaps it is at least as accurate to speak of a vocation's choosing the man, of a call's being given and a man's hearing it, or not hearing it. And maybe that is the place to start: the business of listening and hearing."

Hearing and listening begins when we can be quiet with God. Instead of throwing questions at him, I find more answers by spending some time just being with him, listening.

When I see my daily life as that which God has called me to do, it is easier to make all of my time God's time. All of my words can be his words, even if they are not about him or about my spiritual life. When I live intentionally, with purpose, both the busyness and the boredom give way to peace because I am fulfilling God's call on my life.

"And whatever you do, whether in word or deed, do it all in the name of the Lord Jesus, giving thanks to God the Father through him," Paul writes in Colossians 3:17. When I first studied this verse, I thought: *There's enough societal pressure to "do it all." Now I'm under some sort of religious pressure that says I'm to do it all "in the name of the Lord"?*

And yet this is the heart of hearing his whisper in the chaos of my life: to do all that I do in his name. Although I sometimes wish I could, I cannot withdraw from life's obligations entirely, so I must change my thinking about them. By changing my perspective, I can take what were distractions from my connection with God and turn them into new ways to interact with God.

"We must try to converse with God in little ways while we do our work; not in memorized prayer, not trying to recite previously formed thoughts," writes Brother Lawrence in *The Practice of the Presence of God.* "Rather, we should purely and simply reveal our hearts as the words come to us."

In other words, Brother Lawrence cultivated an ongoing conversation with God. I may be able to do this at times, but my work so often seems to distract me. My kids, my writing (even if it's about spiritual things), even my ministry volunteerism, distract me from conversation with God, from spiritual connection. In order to maintain my connection with God, I need to change the way I look at all of my work, from making a casserole to writing an article. My vocation can and should be a vital part of my life, not something that I simply endure until I can get to Friday and "really live."

I do not limit the term *vocation* to paid employment. Rather, I mean one's life work, whether it is volunteer work or a highly paid profession, whether it is in the church or the home or in the marketplace. If we are at home with children, that is one component, and a rather sizable one, of our life's work. And for now, that may be enough. Raising children is an honorable and heroic vocation.

But sometimes, if we listen carefully, God may be calling us to more than that. He may want us to be home caring for our family, but that does not exempt us from caring for our neighbors. We may be shepherding our children spiritually, but it may be that God wants us to shepherd other people, perhaps from our neighborhood or our church, as well.

Finding our place in the church and the world, as well as the family, is part of what we should consider when trying to determine our calling.

In addition to mothering, my work also includes another part: the craft of writing, without which the other parts of my vocational world don't make any sense. Writing, for me, is both craft and art, a means of making a living and at once an essential element of living. At this season, because my children are small and need a lot of my time, the passion I have for writing far outweighs the time I have for it. But that doesn't mean I should give up on it or file it away under "someday." I am called to love and care for my family, to serve my church, to write, and above all, to live in God's presence. I need to order my life in such a way that I can be obedient to God's call on all of my life, not just one part of it.

Seasons of Life

Because I have small children and have chosen to be at home with them, that really is a big part of my "calling," at least in this season of my life. The writing I do is also part of my calling, as far as I can tell. I don't write just to give myself something else to do besides change diapers. I feel it is what God, by giving me certain gifts and strong desires, has assigned me.

When my children are grown, I do not want to say, "Ah, now that distraction is out of my way, I can get on with finding my purpose in life." Nor do I want to say, "Now that my children are out of my house, I have no purpose left."

We are called to the place we are for a season. But we need to be aware that the season will end, that life is a series of changes. We need to strike a balance between living in the moment and preparing for the next season of our lives. I think it is actually easier to live in the present if we remember that the present situation will not last very long.

I say that I believe it's a ministry of utmost importance to disciple young children and more than a full-time job to run a house and care for young children. I say it; I tell it to others. So why have I sometimes felt obligated to be involved with several ministries at my church? Some bring me closer to God; some distract me from him. Yet like most mothers I wrestle with guilt about how much I am "serving" God. Mothers of school-aged children who do not work outside of the home often feel a similar pressure to volunteer for everything from the PTA to Girl Scouts. It's hard to argue with the voice on the phone that says, "Since you don't work, I'm sure you have time to make two dozen phone calls for the soccer club, bake two dozen cookies for the bake sale . . ."

But as important as it is to "do" everything I do for God, it is even more important to "be with" God and allow him to be with me. When I live in the present and stay mindful of the delicate balance I must strike between doing and being, my connection with him is stronger.

I occasionally do some writing for my church. One morning I was hurrying to get ready to go into the church office for a meeting on a brochure I was writing. My kids would spend the morning in the church nursery.

The hour before I left was full of trying to pack both the diaper bag and my briefcase, making sure the sippy cups and computer disks each got in the right place, getting sleepy kids dressed, finding shoes and coats, and asking myself repeatedly, *Why is just walking out the door so hard?*

As I searched for my son's other shoe and comforted my daughter, who had overslept and was doing some major whining because she just wasn't ready to do anything but drink her orange juice and stare at *Sesame Street,* I thought to myself, *Why do I even bother to try to do anything other than just take care of these two little people? Why am I going to a meeting at 9 a.m.? It would be a lot easier to just sit here in my bathrobe and drink coffee and sing along with Elmo.*

Sometimes trying to do things other than just mothering seems like such a hassle. I work hard enough around here. I don't need to do other things to serve the church or other people. Why bother?

Why? Because sometimes it feels like too much to care for my kids, and sometimes it just isn't enough. Balancing their interests and mine is hard, but I think I'm a better mom when I have some other things in my life. But there is more to it than just balancing.

When I listen carefully to God's whisper, I hear him calling me to love my family and serve them. But when I go into solitude and get uncomfortably quiet with him, I also hear him telling me "fan into flame the gift that is in you." And one of the gifts he has put in me is the ability to use the written word to point people toward him. I'm not saying that to brag. My life would be simpler if I didn't feel compelled to write. But if I leave that gift unopened or undeveloped, I have been disobedient and, ironically, unfulfilled. If I ignore the other components of my calling, my family may get more of my time, but they get more time with a crabby person who is frustrated because she is not using some of the gifts God gave her and called her to use.

Putting Your Soul into It

I love to sing, and for many years I thought of "worship" of God as singing or perhaps praying prayers of adoration to him. Good start, but a rather narrow definition. Then I studied Romans 12:1: "Therefore, I urge you, brothers, in view of God's mercy, to offer your bodies as living sacrifices, holy and pleasing to God—this is your spiritual act of worship."

I had always thought that verse was referring to sexual purity or perhaps just keeping your body healthy through diet and exercise. But I began to see that living sacrifices were acts you did with your body. Daily chores around the house, caring for children or other people, interacting with your co-workers or neighbors—every act of service can be an act of worship.

"We tend to think of the body and its functions as only a hindrance to our spiritual calling, with no positive role in our redemption or in our participation in the government of God. So long as such a view of the body is held, the easy yoke will remain a lovely dream and discipleship a part-time diversion," writes Dallas Willard in *The Spirit of the Disciplines*. The things we do with our body, our physical actions, our work, are essential to our spiritual life.

In the movie *City Slickers* Billy Crystal plays a man who deals with his midlife crisis by visiting a dude ranch where he participates in a cattle drive. Before the trip he is questioning his purpose in life. He realizes that his career as a radio advertising salesperson has very little meaning for him. "What is my job?" he complains to his wife. "I sell advertising time on the radio. So basically, I sell air!"

If we spend most of our waking hours engaged in repetitive, menial tasks that deplete our soul, because we do not see diaper changing or mopping the floor as important or meaningful, we construct barriers that prevent us from hearing God's voice. Caring for young children can be messy, physical work that seems unimportant. But the way that we care for others is critically important. By demonstrating love and care we can show our children what Jesus is like. By seeing ordinary household tasks as opportunities to serve our families as Christ would, not only can we teach our children about God, but our lives will be transformed in the process.

Finding Purpose

To find work, at home or outside of it, that has at least some aspects that we enjoy and an overall purpose that we can see, understand, and support, is necessary for spiritual well being. This is not to say that we will enjoy every part of our work. But alignment with a purpose can transform our perception of the tasks that seem less fulfilling.

Sometimes we can't change our jobs, and we need to let God change our attitudes about them. One of the tasks in my job description that I dislike the most is sweeping the kitchen floor. I sweep it, and moments later it seems to have magically sprouted more crumbs, dirt, Cheerios or whatever. I tend to feel defeated by the floor, and as a result I often let it go until walking across it produces a sort of "crunch, crunch" noise that tells me I can't avoid it any more.

But when I began to think about doing everything for God, I decided to give it the kitchen-floor test. I took out the broom and said, "Right now, God, I'm going to worship you by sweeping this floor." Now, sweeping has not become a magical thing that transports me to the heavenly realms, and I must admit I still don't do it often enough. But if I approach it properly, I can use it as a way to direct my thoughts gently toward God. As I sweep, I thank him that we have a roof over our heads as well as a floor that needs sweeping under our feet. I thank him that my arms and body are strong and healthy enough to take care of my home and that I have these two messy, adorable kids to feed and clean up after.

I tried this with other not-so-pleasant tasks. Have you ever tried to change a dirty diaper as an act of service not only to the diaper wearer but to the Creator as well? This certainly puts a new spin on Jesus' words: "Whatever you did for one of the least of these brothers of mine, you did for me" (Mt 25:40). Certainly this is on my growing edge, but the closer I get to potty training my son, the easier this is becoming!

What He Whispers
Hearing God's whisper through the chaos of life is not easy. When our work is confined to the home, and we receive no

financial compensation for it, finding our sense of purpose is difficult. If we work outside the home and are trying to balance outside pressures with our family's needs, it's hard to remember what's most important, because it all feels urgent.

Even if we take the time to sit down and think about the significance of raising the next generation of leaders for the church, our community and the world, we can quickly lose sight of that vision as we are tossed about in the chaos of life's little details.

When you're trying to get supper started and the house picked up before your husband gets home, and the kids are crying or fighting or just hanging on your leg as you limp awkwardly around the kitchen, it's hard to hang on to that vision.

In those chaotic moments it's important to remember that God hears simple prayers just as clearly as he does more carefully composed ones. "God, have mercy on me!" or even "Help!" are a delight to his ears. He not only hears but responds.

In the chaos he whispers, "I am with you." We believe it and have hope.

For Reflection

1. "We tend to think of the body and its functions as only a hindrance to our spiritual calling, with no positive role in our redemption or in our participation in the government of God. So long as such a view of the body is held, the easy yoke will remain a lovely dream and discipleship a part-time diversion," writes Dallas Willard in *The Spirit of the Disciplines*. Do you see your body and your physical actions as a hindrance to your spiritual growth?

Do you agree with Willard? Why or why not?

2. Do you feel that you have a mission, a purpose? What is it? State it clearly in one sentence.

3. Do you spend most of your time in a vocation (either at home or in the marketplace) that seems to you meaningful and fulfilling? If not, why not?

4. Do you feel that the challenges and stresses of your work bring you closer to God, or do they pull you from him? How?

5. As you look back at the journey you've taken by reading this book, what have you learned?

What one or two chapters resonated with you the most?

6. What are two specific steps could you take to begin to better hear God's whisper in the chaos of your life?

For Further Reading

Bonhoeffer, Dietrich. *Life Together.* New York: Harper & Row, 1954.

Brother Lawrence. *The Practice of the Presence of God.* Edited by Harold J. Chadwick. North Brunswick, N.J.: Bridge-Logos, 2000.

Foster, Richard J. *Celebration of Discipline.* San Francisco: Harper & Row, 1978.

———. *Freedom of Simplicity.* San Fransciso: Harper & Row, 1981.

Gire, Ken. *Windows of the Soul.* Grand Rapids, Mich.: Zondervan, 1996.

Nouwen, Henri. *Life of the Beloved.* New York: Crossroad, 1992.

Ortberg, John. *The Life You've Always Wanted.* Grand Rapids, Mich.: Zondervan, 1997.

Tozer, A. W. *The Pursuit of God.* Camp Hill, Penn.: Christian Publications, 1982.

Willard, Dallas. *The Divine Conspiracy.* New York: HarperCollins, 1998.

———. *The Spirit of the Disciplines.* San Francisco: Harper & Row, 1988.